Tastes and Traditions

Dear Lorena,

I still remember your
last stay in Sydney,
hope to see you soon.
If you have any querries
about the recipes just
give me a call 3631732.

love Lila

Tastes and Traditions

CLASSIC COOKING FOR AUSTRALIANS FROM AROUND THE WORLD

Elaine Diamond Lila Cohen

Illustrations by Jessica Watts

Papago

First published 1993 by Papago, P.O. Box 1038, Hunters Hill 2110.
Prepared for publication by David Ell Press Pty Ltd, 95 Beattie Street, Balmain 2041.

National Library of Australia
Cataloguing-in-Publication Data

Diamond, Elaine.
Tastes and traditions: classic cooking for Australians from around the world.

Includes index.
ISBN 0 646 13034 X.

1. Cookery, International. I. Cohen, Lila. II. Watts, Jessica.
III. Title.

641.59

Design by Deborah Brash
Cover design and text artwork by Christie & Eckermann
Illustrations on pages 60, 92 and 113 by Elaine Diamond
Typeset by Post Typesetters
Printed in Hong Kong through Colorcraft Ltd

Contents

For my mother, Leah Green, and
my mother-in-law, Doris Diamond,
whose wonderful traditional cooking
was my inspiration for this book.
E.D.

Acknowledgements

WE would like to thank the many people who have given us advice and help with this book, and especially the following: Pilar Moreno from the Spanish Club, Sydney; Leo Christie and Georgina Diamond; King Fong; Suzie Sternberg from the Bangkok Restaurant, Sydney; Dr Kopi Okato; Saichalee Varnapruk from the Thai Tourist Information Centre; Songsci Foran of the Thai Australian Association of New South Wales; Carl Robinson from the Old Saigon Restaurant, Sydney; Layla Sorfie; Claude Hakim; Paul Maloney; Donato di Giacomo, Lucania Association; Mina Lipo and Carmel Romeo from the Puglia Association; Laura Mecca, Italian Historical Association (Victoria); and Waverley Municipal Library.

Our warmest thanks to Lea Einfeld for her time and patience. She has been responsible for much of the research and organisation of the background material. Her editorial assistance has been invaluable.

'The pleasures of the table remain to console for the loss of country.'

Brillat-Savarin

Introduction

OUR desire to understand contemporary Australian cuisine led us on a voyage of discovery of the way in which our earliest choices of food have been changed. Australia is host to settlers from many parts of the world who have brought with them their special foods which reflect their geography, their history, their religion and their festivals. These folk generally settled in chosen pockets, most of them in Melbourne and Sydney. Thus family ties have been kept, traditions nurtured and traditional foods eaten. Most striking is the connection between the traditional festivals lovingly observed here and the special foods served on these occasions. The presentation of these foods at particular times provides a link with a long heritage and serves in a pragmatic way to revitalise that spiritual legacy.

The Australian palate had been educated to some degree in earlier days by Chinese cooks on the goldfields where small Chinese kitchens sprang up and provided new experiences to compete with roast lamb and damper, by the visits to Europe of wealthy squatters who brought back a taste for the refinements of European cooking and, more recently, by visits to Asia of people who returned seduced by the intricate and spicy dishes of the East.

So our taste buds had been introduced to foreign flavours and were ready for the invasion of new ideas in food brought by settlers from many different parts of the globe and made accessible to all through speciality shops and restaurants.

The coming in the second half of this century of many new peoples meant that they themselves demanded and introduced to the diet of this country a whole new range of flavours and ingredients which found a ready and appreciative response here.

To meet these demands, a host of restaurants and 'take-aways' has proliferated throughout the country. The foods sold by these eateries sometimes bear a poor resemblance to the dishes so carefully created in home kitchens where recipes have been handed down for generations and culinary secrets have often been kept within the family.

Our recipes have come from our own experience, from family and tradition, and from friends among early and recent arrivals. We have not attempted rigid reproductions of any of these recipes, but have sought the essence of the dish, perhaps the main ingredient, and devised more accessible and often simplified versions.

In selecting the styles of cooking to include in this book, we considered those communities who had immigrated to Australia in substantial numbers, who had brought with them the tastes and traditions of their homelands, whose cuisine had made the greatest impact on Australian eating habits and, lastly, those with whom we had some personal contact. From the people we talked to, we could put together a picture of the customs and cuisine brought from many parts of the globe to their new homeland.

We have therefore included seven styles of cooking brought to us from across the seven seas: Italian, Greek, Spanish, Jewish, Middle Eastern, Japanese and Asian. Some you will know well; others you may not be familiar with. We have enjoyed experimenting with the recipes from all of these cultures. We hope that you, too, will find this enjoyable and challenging.

Italian

ORIGINATING from Greek cuisine, Italian food has a long and glorious history. Most everyday dishes are still based on those eaten in ancient Rome. When the Romans were on their victorious marches to conquer new territories, they prepared a gruel of crushed roasted wheat which they called pulmentum or puls. The contemporary equivalent is polenta, made today from maize flour. From the conquered lands they brought back artichokes, cherries, dates and pistachio nuts to add to the Roman diet of beans, cabbage, lettuce, grapes, figs and pears.

During the Renaissance, Italy led the world in its spirit of adventure: in thought, art and cooking, too. Cooks were highly esteemed and positions in the kitchen, highly coveted. Eating became more elegant: the rules of table setting were laid down and Catherine de Medici, who married the King of France, introduced the fork to the French Court! From the New World came new fruits, spices and plants, such as corn. Cooking became more complex and developed into an art form.

The ingredients in Italian cooking today are as varied as the many areas that produce them. All regions, and even cities, have their unique foods. In Lombardy, vegetable soups well-flavoured with herbs, osso bucco and dishes rich in butter are favoured. Venice specialises in fish and seafood. Bologna, in Emilia-Romagna, is noted for its pasta and sausage, and Calabria for eggplant and tuna. Among the desserts originating from particular regions are panettone from Milan, Venetian lemon biscuits, zabaglione from Florence, almond macaroons from Sicily and Genoese marzipan.

Italy has introduced pasta to the world's tables, with a seemingly infinite variety of herb sauces. From Italy, too, have come unique cheeses such as parmesan, gorgonzola, bel paese, mozzarella and mascarpone.

The earliest Italian immigrants arrived in Australia in the middle of the last century. The gold rushes of the 1850s attracted a thousand Italians from Valtellina on the Swiss border to Ballarat and Bendigo in Victoria. Their descendants stayed and formed communities in these centres. The political upheaval leading to the unification of Italy in 1840 caused more Italians to come here. They took up wine production, an industry centuries old in their homeland. At this time, also, the first pasta factory was established at Hepburn in Victoria.

By the first decade of this century, many Italians had left their small towns and villages to join cousins, uncles and neighbours who had already settled into their new life. In 1920, after World War I, they came in large numbers to work on the sugar cane fields in northern New South Wales and Queensland. Some who found their way to Western Australia established vineyards in the Swan Valley. Again, in the aftermath of World War II, they came to escape the devastation in their country.

Today, the largest number of Italian-born people live in Victoria — over 40 per cent of a total of 261,000 in Australia. They prefer to live close to the city centre: in Brunswick in Melbourne and Leichhardt in Sydney, for example, although they also congregate in suburbs such as Keilor, Werribee and Bulleen in Melbourne and Drummoyne in Sydney.

On their arrival in Australia, Italian growers began to produce fruit and vegetables of high quality and of varieties not hitherto seen here, such as zucchini and broccoli. The earliest sausage makers were Italian, and cheesemakers and grocers extended the local eating experience. The Italian influence on our food was revealed early, in our growing taste for spaghetti and tomato sauce. Italian cooks brought their own specialities and have passed these on to their children.

Family life is strong, and wonderful meals are cooked at home and shared with family and friends. But Italians like to meet — and eat — with others from their home towns, and to keep up with local traditions. Wher-

ever they are, there are clubs with busy social and sporting programs. The Italian Social Club in Werribee, a centre for small farming and market gardening since 1927, has over one thousand local members and caters for weddings, dinner dances and sporting events.

The Club Veneto in Bulleen is twenty-four-years-old and has about one thousand eight hundred members, originally from the Veneto area in northern Italy, embracing Venice and Vicenza. Sport is a high priority, as are the meals served here, mostly the popular pasta, veal and chicken dishes. Club Cavour in Carlton is named after a famous statesman, Conte Camillo Benso di Cavour, a leader of the movement for the unification of Italy.

There are over three hundred regional associations in Sydney. A typical example is the Puglia Association in Leichhardt, many of whose members come from the coastal town of Molfetta. The chief products of this area are olives, almonds, figs and prickly pear. We were told that the oil produced at home came straight from the press and was thick, syrupy and fruity. In Australia, they found that the oil was very refined and difficult to get used to. However, they said, their children adapted quickly and now prefer the oils sold here.

Another association in Sydney is Lucania, the old name for Basilicata. From the town of San Fele in this area, two thousand, or one-third, of its inhabitants have settled in the municipality of Drummoyne, which has been officially named sister city to San Fele.

Festivals celebrated in Italy are remembered and observed here with great sentiment, along with the foods symbolically related to them. On Palm Sunday a special lunch is served, often pasta with ricotta. On Good Friday, the bitter leaves of rape are eaten. They are boiled, and oil, lemon juice and, sometimes, anchovies added. Broccoli leaves or endive can be used instead. Come Easter Sunday and meat can be eaten again. A great delicacy is Il Capretto, baby goat or kid. At the Puglia Club we were given a traditional recipe, but we have substituted lamb as it is more readily available here. On Easter Monday family and friends go for picnics where cake called Colomba is served. It is a yeast cake, filled with sultanas and candied citrus peel, in the shape of a dove, the symbol of peace. A popular Easter dessert is Zuppa Inglese.

On Christmas Eve, before Midnight Mass, only light food is eaten: fritto misto (fried mixed seafoods), fritella or panzarotti. These are rice fritters, served hot and dusted with sugar. Rice is the symbol of life and immortality.

On New Year's Eve, because twelve is a mystical number for Italians, often twelve courses are served. These can include soups, pasta, sausages, many kinds of seafood, lasagna, ravioli, poultry, game, beef and lentils with pigs' trotters (for good luck).

A traditional cake served at Christmas and New Year is panettone. *Larousse Gastronomique* tells a charming legend about this name, derived from Pane di Tonio. Tonio, a poor baker from Milan, had a pretty daughter whom a young nobleman wanted to

141
BUON APPETITO
PASTA

marry. But Tonio could not afford the mandatory dowry. Instead, he provided all the ingredients to make a splendid cake. He made a fortune from this cake and his daughter made a good match.

Weddings and christenings are lavish affairs. The wedding feast is grand, with many courses. Cassata features regularly, together with pastel-coloured, sugar-coated almonds. The meal ends with liqueurs, such as sambucca, and amoretti biscuits.

The Blessing of the Fleet is celebrated in Sydney on the last day of Carnivale in October. A procession to Darling Harbour moves off after a mass in St Mary's Cathedral and every association taking part displays its banner. The statue of 'Madonna of the Sea' is carried high on the shoulders of the fishermen. The boats are blessed at Darling Harbour, then a party is held in a huge tent. Lots of pizza, fresh pasta and capsicum stuffed with rice are served.

As well as the main religious festivals, saints' days are marked in some clubs by fairs with stalls selling regional foods and crafts. To celebrate their patron saint's day, Sydney's Drummoyne community holds a similar fair in Five Dock Park. Hundreds come along to eat and buy. Nor are secular national days ignored. Clubs often combine to celebrate 'Festa Republica' — Italian Republic Day — marking the inauguration of the Republic in 1947. In Melbourne the community takes over the Moonee Valley racecourse.

Leichhardt is the heart of Italian food in Sydney. Here are colourful and authentic restaurants and food shops. Butchers offer a seemingly infinite variety of sausages, prosciutto, venison (dried and cured), buffalo, wild duck, pheasant, guinea fowl, pigeon and baby goat. Bakers make and sell foccacia, rosettas (little rolls) and pizza bases. At fruit shops you can buy different sizes of chestnuts, fresh olives, rape, red broccoli, fresh quinces and borlotti beans. At delicatessens there are locally made cheeses and sausages, anchovies, pickled vegetables, mineral waters, tomato pastes, pastas and aromatic coffees.

Lygon Street, Carlton, now resembles a street in any major Italian city: bars, restaurants, pasta shops, coffee shops, delicatessens and gelateria offer a wealth of Italian foodstuffs. You can now cook for yourself the food to be enjoyed in Carlton's or Leichhardt's innumerable Italian restaurants where Italian is the flavour of every month.

PAPPA AL POMODORO

This is a hearty and satisfying soup which is simple to make. It originated in Tuscany where it is considered a waste to throw away stale bread. The bread must be coarse country bread or the soup will be mushy. The beef stock gives this soup its rich flavour.

• SERVES 6 •

½ cup olive oil
3 cloves garlic, chopped
3 sage leaves, chopped
3 tablespoons chopped thyme
250 g stale Italian bread, thinly sliced
1 kg peeled ripe tomatoes
6 cups meat stock
salt and pepper

Heat the oil in a saucepan. Add the garlic, sage leaves and thyme, and sauté until the garlic turns golden. Add the sliced bread and brown on both sides. Purée the tomatoes and add to the bread mixture. Cook for 5 minutes. Add the beef stock and bring to the boil. Reduce the heat and simmer, covered, for 30–40 minutes, stirring occasionally. Season to taste.

FIORI DI ZUCCHINI FRITTI

This dish often features on restaurant menus and is an example of how Australian cooking has been enriched by Italian influences. It is now possible to obtain fresh zucchini flowers from Italian growers.

• SERVES 6 •

100 g mozzarella or bocconcini
2 tablespoons grated parmesan
6 anchovy fillets
12 zucchini flowers

Batter

1 cup beer
150 g plain flour
1 tablespoon olive oil
2 eggs, separated

In a food processor combine the mozzarella, parmesan and anchovies. Gently remove the centres from the flowers, trying not to tear the petals. Push the mixture into each flower, pressing the top together.

Make the batter by adding the egg yolks to the flour, oil and beer. Leave in the refrigerator for 1 hour. Before using, add the stiffly beaten egg whites.

Dip the flowers into the batter and fry in hot oil until crisp and golden. Drain on paper towels and serve.

Rigatoni con Spinaci e Ricotta

Short hollow pasta, topped with fried ricotta and spinach, is another simple, yet delicious, dish. It is important to drain the ricotta well before frying.

• SERVES 4 •

200 g ricotta
½ cup olive oil
1 bunch English spinach, chopped
300 g rigatoni
salt and pepper
chilli flakes

First drain the ricotta, then cut it into 3 cm cubes. Fry in the oil on all sides, lifting them gently and taking care not to break them. Put aside.

Remove three-quarters of the oil and toss the spinach for 1 minute until it is just cooked.

Boil and drain the rigatoni, arrange on a plate and cover with the cooked spinach. Place the fried ricotta on top of the spinach. Sprinkle with salt, pepper and chilli flakes.

Fusilli al Mascarpone e Limone

This is a creamy rich sauce, with the tanginess of lemon zest, which is easy and quick to make. Any shape of pasta will suffice.

• SERVES 4 •

500 g fusilli
250 ml cream
2 tablespoons mascarpone
60 g butter
120 g parmesan, freshly grated
grated rind of 2 lemons

Boil the pasta in boiling, salted water until it is *al dente*. While this is cooking, heat the cream with the mascarpone, butter, lemon zest and parmesan.

Drain the pasta and turn on to a serving dish. Toss in the sauce, mix thoroughly and serve.

BRUSCHETTA

Bruschetta is an Italian country-style bread that is grilled, rubbed with garlic and brushed with olive oil. It can also be covered with a variety of toppings. The secret to a delicious bruschetta is to use the finest olive oil. Vine-ripened tomatoes which have been slowly baked in the oven make an easy and delicious topping.

• SERVES 4 •

4 medium-sized tomatoes
2 tablespoons olive oil
8 slices bread
2 cloves garlic, crushed
basil leaves
2 tablespoons balsamic vinegar
salt and pepper

An hour before assembling the toast, cut the tomatoes in half and remove all the seeds. Place them on a rack with the cut sides upwards, brush them with olive oil and bake slowly in the oven for 1 hour. Grill or toast the bread and, while still warm, rub it with crushed garlic, then brush with olive oil. Tear the basil leaves and scatter them over the bread. Place the baked tomatoes on top. Sprinkle with salt, pepper and balsamic vinegar.

RISOTTO AL FUNGHI FRESCHI

Risotto is a Northern Italian speciality, and the king of rice dishes. Like most dishes it needs quality ingredients and correct cooking to ensure success. To make a terrific risotto you should use Arborio rice. It needs slower cooking to absorb the flavours and yet retain its firmness. Use unsalted butter (not margarine or oil), freshly grated parmesan cheese, dry wine, a heavy pot and a wooden spoon.

• SERVES 6 •

750 g field mushrooms
8 tablespoons butter
1 large onion, chopped
2 cups Arborio rice
¾ cup dry white wine
6–8 cups beef stock
¾ cup grated parmesan
2 tablespoons chopped parsley

Separate the caps from the stems of the mushrooms. Wipe the caps and slice. Melt 6 tablespoons of the butter in a heavy pot. Add the chopped onion and cook until transparent. Add the rice and keep stirring until it is all coated in the hot butter.

When the rice has a shiny glow, add the wine and continue to cook slowly until it has evaporated. Add a cupful of the hot stock to the rice and keep stirring until it has been absorbed. Continue to add the stock cupful by cupful, stirring all the time. This should take about 15 minutes. Spread the mushroom caps over the rice and fold in gently. Continue to add the stock gradually, waiting each time until it has been absorbed. This should take another 10 minutes. (The rice should be cooked *al dente.*)

Turn off the heat and add the grated parmesan, parsley and the rest of the butter. Put the lid on the saucepan for 2 minutes and then serve.

CALZONE

A pizza, stuffed with a variety of ingredients, is a traditional recipe of Puglia, a region of South-Eastern Italy, on the Adriatic. The dough is made without yeast and it rises due to the natural fermentation of flour. As a result, it is not as 'bready' as a conventional pizza. The dough pockets, after being filled and sealed, are fried in olive oil. They then become a delicious mixture of textures and flavours, crisp on the outside and soft and moreish on the inside.

• SERVES 4 •

Dough

350 g flour
1 teaspoon salt
200 ml warm water
1 tablespoon olive oil

Filling

500 g tomatoes
2 tablespoons chopped onion
1 tablespoon crushed garlic
2 tablespoons olive oil
salt and pepper
oregano
250 g mozzarella
olive oil for frying

Sift the flour and salt onto a bench top and make a hole in the centre. Pour the water and oil into the hole. Mix thoroughly and knead well. Leave the dough to rest in a warm place for two hours.

Peel the tomatoes and remove the seeds. Fry the onions and garlic in the 2 tablespoons of oil until soft, then add the chopped tomatoes. Cook for 15 minutes. Add salt, pepper and oregano and cook for a further 15 minutes. Put the mixture aside until cool.

Roll out the dough into discs, 12 cm in diameter. Place 2 tablespoons of the tomato mixture in the centre of each disc. Place a slice of mozzarella on top of the tomatoes. Fold each disc in half and seal the edges. Fry in hot oil until the pastry is lightly browned.

TORTA DI PATATE

Potato pie is a perfect picnic dish. It is yet another variation on the combination of tomatoes, mozzarella, oregano and olive oil so loved by the Italians. Here, instead of pastry, potatoes are used as the base.

• SERVES 6 •

500 g potatoes
2 tablespoons olive oil
salt and pepper
180 g mozzarella
250 g tomatoes
oregano
8 anchovy fillets

Boil the potatoes. When cool, force them through a sieve. Mix them with half the oil, add salt and pepper to taste and spread mixture on the base of a greased pizza tray. Cover with sliced mozzarella.

Remove the seeds and skin from the tomatoes and drain them as much as possible. Slice the tomatoes and place on top of the mozzarella. Sprinkle with oregano and arrange the anchovies. Drizzle with the remainder of the olive oil and bake in a preheated oven for 20 minutes.

AGNELLO AL FORNO

At Easter young goat, or kid, is traditionally served. We have adapted an old recipe from Puglia by substituting lamb for the baby goat. The olive tree branch gives this dish a delightful fragrance but if it is difficult to find you can use bay leaves instead.

● SERVES 4 ●

150 g onions, chopped
oil for frying
400 g lamb, cubed
150 ml white wine
300 g potatoes, chopped in quarters
pinch of chilli flakes, parsley, nutmeg
salt and pepper
100 g pecorino, grated
small olive tree branch

Fry onions until tender. Add lamb and fry until sealed on all sides. Pour in the wine and simmer for half an hour until some of the fluid has evaporated. Remove the meat and cook the potatoes in the same saucepan. When they are half cooked, put the lamb back into the saucepan. Add the spices and salt and pepper to taste, cover the saucepan and allow to cook for a further 30 minutes.

Place the cooked lamb and potatoes in an ovenproof dish, sprinkle with grated pecorino and place the olive tree branch on top. Cover with silver foil and bake in the oven for 30 minutes.

QUAGLIE CON POLENTA

The quickly seared quails, previously marinated in red wine and olive oil, and deliciously scented with juniper berries and rosemary, are a perfect companion to the creamy polenta.

● SERVES 4 ●

8 quails
½ cup red wine
¼ cup olive oil
2 sprigs rosemary
8 juniper berries
1 cup polenta
2½ cups boiling salted water
2 tablespoons double cream
salt and pepper

Ask the butcher to cut and splay the quails. Mix the red wine, olive oil, juniper berries and rosemary. Place quails in the marinade, making sure they are covered. Leave in refrigerator overnight.

Pour the polenta into the boiling salted water. Whisk vigorously to prevent lumps forming. Cook in a non-stick saucepan for 30–50 minutes, stirring from time to time. If the polenta becomes lumpy, blend it in a food processor for a few seconds. Finally, add the double cream.

Meanwhile, heat the griller and cook the quails, 10 minutes on each side. Arrange the grilled quails on the bed of creamy polenta. Season to taste.

SARDE IN VINO BIANCO

Sardines steeped in white wine marinade make a delightful summer dish.

• SERVES 4 •

400 g sardines	*100 g onions, sliced*
flour	*200 ml white wine*
oil for frying	*salt and pepper*

Dip the clean sardines in flour. Fry them in the oil and let them drain on a rack. In the same pan, fry the onions until soft, add the white wine and boil until two-thirds of the liquid has evaporated. Place the sardines in a dish, season to taste, cover them with the marinade and serve the next day.

INSALATA INDIVIA CON GORGONZOLA

Many Italian dishes are simple to prepare. What makes them so delicious is the freshest of ingredients and imaginative combinations. In this recipe we have substituted Belgian endive for the bitter leaves of rape.

• SERVES 4 •

4 small Belgian endive	*salt and pepper*
100 g gorgonzola	*2 tablespoons olive oil*
50 g walnuts	*1 tablespoon white wine vinegar*

Arrange the endive on a plate. Scatter the gorgonzola on top, then the walnuts. Sprinkle with salt and pepper. Finally, pour over the olive oil and white wine vinegar.

Insalata di Tonno con Borlotti

This dish is often made with canned tuna and dried beans. Australia produces one of the best catches of tuna in the world, and fresh borlotti beans are available in autumn. When made with fresh ingredients, this Italian speciality will delight even the most jaded palate.

• SERVES 4 •

200 g fresh tuna
small bunch of fresh basil
2–3 cloves garlic
4 tablespoons olive oil
200 g borlotti beans
100 g Spanish onions
1 tablespoon balsamic vinegar
salt and pepper

Tear about 6 basil leaves and squash the garlic. Pour 2 tablespoons of oil over the basil and garlic. Cut the tuna into small steaks and cover with the above marinade. Leave for 2 hours.

Boil the borlotti beans for 15 minutes until still slightly crisp. Drain and cool. Grill the marinated pieces of tuna very lightly, leaving them slightly rare. Thinly slice the onions. Arrange the beans on a plate, scatter the onions over the beans, then place the grilled tuna on top. Season to taste. Sprinkle with the remaining oil and vinegar. Garnish with basil.

BUDINO DI PANETTONE

Leftover panettone makes the perfect ingredient for this delicious pudding, richly flavoured with marsala.

• SERVES 6 •

4 slices panettone, broken into pieces
70 g candied fruit, diced
50 g sultanas
4 eggs
100 g sugar
½ litre milk
3 tablespoons marsala

Lightly grease a shallow oval ovenproof dish, approximately 24 cm long. Place in it alternate layers of panettone, candied fruit and sultanas. Do not pack down. Whisk together lightly the eggs and the sugar, then whisk in the milk and marsala. Pour this mixture into the baking dish and allow to rest for at least 1 hour. Bake in a preheated oven, 180°C, for about 30 minutes. The pudding is ready when the blade of a knife, inserted in the centre, comes out clean. Allow to cool before serving.

TORTA AL MARSALA CON FRAGOLE

This is a light and delicate tart that is best eaten on the day it is made.

• SERVES 6 •

Pastry

150 g butter
100 g sugar
200 g flour
50 g almonds, finely ground
1 egg yolk

Filling

5 egg yolks
100 g sugar
50 ml marsala
400 g strawberries

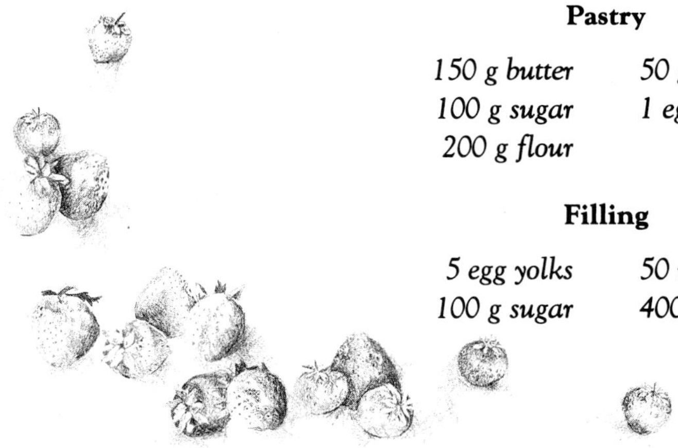

To make the pastry, combine the butter and the sugar until the mixture resembles breadcrumbs. Add the flour and ground almonds, then the egg yolk. Mix together gently and form into a ball. Leave it to rest in the refrigerator for 2 hours. Roll out the pastry and line a greased shallow 24 cm cake tin. Cover with greaseproof paper, fill with baking weights and bake for 20 minutes, or until it becomes crisp. Leave to cool.

Place the egg yolks and sugar in a deep glass bowl. Stir with a wooden spoon until the mixture becomes fluffy. Add the marsala and place the bowl on top of a double boiler. Stir the mixture until it coats the spoon. Do not allow it to overheat. Remove from stove and allow to cool for about 1 hour. Pour the cold zabaglione into the cooled tart shell and bake at 180°C until set. When the tart is cold, arrange fresh strawberries on top.

Cassata alla Siciliana

Ricotta is used a great deal in Italian cooking, both in sweet and savoury dishes. It is a very soft, fresh cheese. Here is our version of this famous Sicilian dessert.

• SERVES 6 •

12 savoiardi biscuits
½ cup brandy
500 g ricotta
180 g icing sugar
1 teaspoon vanilla essence
4 tablespoons mixed candied fruit, chopped
4 tablespoons cooking chocolate, chopped
4 tablespoons maraschino liqueur
icing sugar and candied fruit for decoration

Line the bottom of a rectangular dish (25 cm long) with 6 savoiardi biscuits. Soak them with half of the brandy.

Sieve ricotta into a bowl and beat in the icing sugar and vanilla to make a smooth, light, fluffy mixture. Fold in the candied fruit, chocolate and liqueur.

Place the ricotta mixture on top of the biscuits. Sprinkle brandy on the remaining 6 biscuits and place them on top of the ricotta mixture. Dust with icing sugar and decorate with candied fruit.

Torta di Fichi e Cioccolato

This sweet cake, made with dried figs and chocolate icing, is popular at Christmas because it is very easy to make and offers variety during the festive season.

• SERVES 6 •

1 cup red wine
2 tablespoons sugar
1 teaspoon cinnamon
600 g large dried figs
100 g dark chocolate (couverture)
1 tablespoon clarified butter

Place the wine, sugar and cinnamon in a saucepan. Bring to the boil and stir until the sugar has dissolved. Poach the figs for 10 minutes in this mixture. Remove the figs and leave them to cool. Reduce the sauce until 3 tablespoons remain.

Arrange the figs tightly in a shallow, round earthenware dish, cover with the wine sauce and bake in a preheated oven at 150°C for 30 minutes.

Melt the chocolate in a double saucepan and add the clarified butter. When the baked figs are cool, cover them with lukewarm chocolate icing. Allow the chocolate icing to set firmly before serving. Slice into wedges and serve with cream or fresh mascarpone.

Greek

EVEN in Ancient Greece, great occasions were celebrated with feasting. The climate and proximity to the sea provided abundant food. Wine flowed and care was lavished on a variety of dishes.

When trade opened up between the mainland and the islands of the Aegean, elements of the different cuisines were exchanged and the resulting recipes survive today.

In the thirteenth century, Turkey invaded and conquered the Middle East and introduced to Greece the soldiers' art of roasting meats on spits and skewers.

Traditions based on religion and folklore are still strong in Greece and also among the Greek population in Australia today, and special occasions are marked by the serving of traditional foods.

The first Greeks arrived in Sydney at the end of the nineteenth century. They left a poor homeland for a land of opportunity, with the hope of finding work and sending money home to help members of their family who were unable to leave.

One of the largest waves of emigrants followed the First World War when the Turks were at war with the Greeks in Asia Minor and the islands nearby. Many came from Ithaca and Kythera, and nearly the whole population of Castellorizo migrated in 1922. Another major migration occurred after World War II, and again in 1956 when Nasser came to power in Egypt.

Those Greeks who arrived in Australia before World War II often opened small businesses; the post-War arrivals found work in the factories in their thousands. Pre-War, they came from the islands of Greece; post-War, they came mainly from the mainland and from areas, such as Egypt, Cyprus and Asia Minor. Political troubles in Cyprus and the growing Islamic influence in Nasser's Egypt of the 'fifties, together with Government assistance, boosted the number of Greek emigrants. But the strongest pull of all was the system of chain migration by which earlier arrivals in Australia sponsored relatives and friends from their home regions.

The Greek population in Australia tends to preserve the values and customs which they brought with them even though these mores are constantly evolving in their homeland. They adhere particularly strongly to their Greek Orthodox faith, their language and their family ties.

As a seafaring nation, the Greeks continue to ply their trade as fishermen, wholesale fish merchants or as owners of almost every fish and chip shop in Australia. Melbourne's Prahran and Victoria Markets, and the fish market in Sydney, stock a wealth of seafood, often picturesquely displayed.

Because food is almost a ritual in Greece, the newly arrived Greeks also moved into other areas of the food business. They opened bars and cafes as they were businesses they could operate without having to master the English language and they were also willing to work the required long hours.

One of the first milk bars in Sydney was the 'Black and White' in Martin Place which became a Sydney institution. The owner, Mick Adams, employed many young Greeks whom he trained, as in a school. Here they learned the trade and then opened their own milk bars. Most country towns had a Greek cafe or milk bar, not serving Greek food but rather steak and eggs. Today Greeks run coffee lounges, fish shops, cake shops,

butcher shops, restaurants — anything to do with food. Among foods introduced to Australia by the Greeks are yoghurt, olives, olive oil and, of course, Greek salad.

In Sydney, the Athenium Club in Castlereagh Street also became an institution. It introduced cheap food with a difference to the community. Greek salad and spaghetti were great favourites.

The largest Greek community outside Greece is in Melbourne. They have moved through the port areas to Richmond and Prahran. Swan Street, Richmond and the section of Lonsdale Street, between Russell and Swanston Streets, known affectionately as the 'Greek spot', are lined with Greek restaurants, delicatessens and pastry shops, with impressive displays of traditional cakes, large slabs of halva and innumerable varieties of olives.

Both in Melbourne and Sydney, the Greek community has created a lifestyle reminiscent of life in Greece. They celebrate with great pride their National Independence Day on 25 March. In Melbourne, the Greek section of Lonsdale Street is closed off and there are parades and ceremonies, dancing, entertainment and terrific Greek food for sale.

They follow their own football teams and have many communal outings and celebrations, meeting at various clubs and coffee shops to enjoy coffee and cake. Greek weddings are legendary, with no expense spared, and they have a charming custom of giving gifts of sugar-coated almonds to the guests.

Easter is their most important religious festival. At midnight on Easter Saturday bells ring and candles are lit for the celebration of the Resurrection or Anastasi, as it is called in Greece.

It is traditional at Easter to hard boil eggs and dye them red. Friends then knock each other's eggs, while repeating 'Christ is risen'.

A traditional meal is eaten, including Easter soup, called mayeritsa. This consists of lamb, liver, shallots, rice, lemon and eggs. A popular soup for the same occasion is egg and lemon soup.

On Easter Sunday the centrepiece is a spit-roasted lamb. Usually the spit is hired for the occasion. For a smaller gathering, a boned and butterflied leg of lamb can be substituted. Salads accompany the lamb. Easter bread, which is plaited in a round or cylindrical shape, is served, with the coloured eggs tucked inside. Easter bread is sold at Greek cake shops.

At Christmas and New Year there is again much food preparation and baking. On New Year's Eve, vasilopita, or St Basil's cake, is served. A coin is hidden inside the cake and whoever finds it is guaranteed a year's good luck.

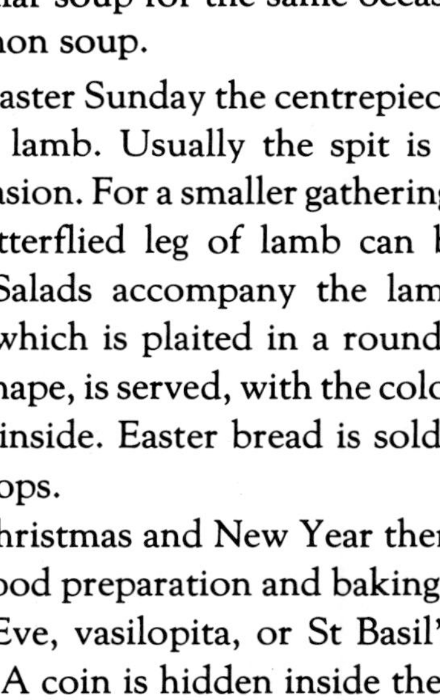

THE GREEK DELI
TAVERNA
B.Y.O
2413734
EAT IN OR
TAKE AWAY.
THE GREEK DELI
TAVERNA BYO
RESTAURANT

Instead of birthdays, name day or saint's day is celebrated. If one is named after a saint, such as Saint Nicholas or Saint Andrew, one is 'at home' on that saint's day. Friends call and are served coffee and sweatmeats.

Nowadays, a meal here starts with appetizers called mezzedes. Mezzedes may be taramasalata, stuffed vine leaves (dolmades) or a dip, made of yoghurt, cucumber and garlic, called tzatziki, and, of course, olives. Ouzo, the Greek apéritif, or retsina is served with these appetizers.

Next, lamb or fish is served with vegetables. Aubergines and zucchini are cooked in many original ways. Moussaka is a delicious Greek speciality in which layers of fried aubergine and minced lamb are covered with a béchamel sauce and baked in the oven. Rice or potatoes are always served as an accompaniment.

Lemons are often used as an ingredient in marinades for vegetables and meat, and avgolemono, a lemon and egg sauce, as its name suggests, is very popular with fish.

Greek people are great cheese eaters and cheese is usually served with the meal. Fetta is the most famous of all. It is made from sheep's milk, shaped into round or square blocks, then stored in wooden barrels. Fetta is white with a piquant flavour. Kefalotiri is a hard cheese, with a sharp, salty taste, made from sheep and goat's milk. Kasseri, a semi-hard cheese, is yellowish white in colour and strong tasting. Kefalogravieri is the Greek version of gruyère, rather sweet and highly regarded.

To complete the meal, very sweet black coffee is served with sticky sweet pastries. Baklava, walnut cakes and honey puffs are among the most popular of a large variety of desserts.

Everywhere, today, you can find kalamata olives, fetta cheese and filo pastry, but the greatest variety of Greek food is still to be found in the delicatessens, cake, butcher and fish shops of Marrickville and Newtown in Sydney, and Richmond and Lonsdale Street in Melbourne. During the day, the women shop, and after five o'clock in the afternoon, the men sit and sip Greek coffee, listen to music and exchange news and views.

AVGOLEMONO

This famous Greek soup is the start to many a festive meal. Do not allow the soup to boil after the egg has been added, otherwise it will curdle.

• SERVES 6 •

6 cups tasty chicken stock
1 cup rice
1 cup of diced steamed chicken
juice of 1 large lemon (to taste)
4 eggs, beaten
1 teaspoon grated lemon rind
coarsely ground black pepper

Bring chicken stock to the boil, add rice and cook for 12 minutes. Add cooked chicken and lemon juice. Pour some of the soup liquid into the beaten eggs, then add this mixture to the soup. Ladle into serving bowls and sprinkle with pepper and grated lemon rind.

FASOLATHA

This hearty traditional soup is extremely popular in Greece and Australia. It is simple to make and the vegetables we have suggested can be replaced by whatever is in the fridge. Serve with crusty bread.

• SERVES 6–8 •

350 g white beans, soaked overnight in cold water
500 g onions or leeks, chopped
2 garlic cloves, finely chopped
3 tablespoons olive oil
6 stalks celery, chopped
250 g carrots, chopped
6 stems parsley, chopped
2 bay leaves
1 chilli, chopped
4 tomatoes, peeled and chopped
salt and pepper

Drain the white beans, add just enough water to cover and boil for 10 minutes. Drain again, cover with water and bring back to the boil. Cover with lid and simmer for 1 hour, or until tender.

Meanwhile, sauté the onions and garlic in the olive oil until light brown. Add the diced celery, carrots, parsley, bay leaves and chilli, and sauté for a further 3 minutes. Drain the cooked white beans and add to them the sautéed vegetables and the chopped tomatoes. Cover with water and bring to the boil. Reduce heat and simmer, covered, for 15 minutes until the beans are tender but not mushy. Add salt and pepper to taste.

TZATZIKI

This traditional appetizer is refreshing and can be made with low caloric yoghurt or goat's milk yoghurt.

• SERVES 6 •

1 small cucumber
1 cup thick yoghurt
1 teaspoon olive oil
1 teaspoon lemon juice
1 clove garlic, crushed
salt and pepper

Peel and grate the cucumber and leave it in a colander to drain off some of the moisture. Place the yoghurt in a serving bowl, add all other ingredients and mix well. Serve chilled, accompanied by toasted pitta bread.

KOULOKETHI ME CAROTA PITA

Cracked wheat is a popular ingredient in many Greek dishes. It gives this delicious pie a nutty flavour. The base is tissue thin pastry, filo, which can be bought in Greek grocery shops and supermarkets.

• SERVES 6 •

1 packet filo pastry
100 g melted butter
250 g zucchinis
150 g carrots
½ cup chopped green onions
1 tablespoon chopped fresh coriander
½ cup cracked wheat
2 eggs
1 cup creamy natural yoghurt
salt and pepper

Soak cracked wheat in water overnight and drain.

Cut pastry to line a round 24 cm pie dish. Layer 8 sheets, one on top of the other, brushing each sheet with melted butter. Grate zucchinis and carrots coarsely. Mix with green onion and coriander.

Sprinkle the cracked wheat on the bottom of the pastry-lined dish and add the vegetable mixture. Whisk the eggs with the yoghurt, add salt and pepper to taste and pour on top. Bake in a preheated oven at 180°C for 40 minutes.

DOLMADES

Dolmades are often part of small appetizers known as mezzedes. If you are able to obtain fresh vine leaves, your dolmades will be more authentic. Otherwise, use the bottled variety.

• SERVES 10 •

50 vine leaves
1 cup virgin olive oil
1¾ cups onions, finely chopped
1 cup shallots, mainly green stems, finely chopped
½ cup dill, finely chopped
½ cup mint, finely chopped
1 cup rice
salt and pepper
juice of 1 lemon

Pour boiling water over the vine leaves to soften. Drain and cool. Mix all the ingredients together, except the lemon juice, and place a spoonful of this mixture in the middle of each leaf. Wrap them up into parcels. Place in a non-stick saucepan and put a plate on top of the leaves to stop them from unfolding. Barely cover them with water and lemon juice and boil slowly until all the water has been absorbed and the rice, cooked. Allow to cool.

ARNI PSITO STA KARVOVNA

Traditionally a whole lamb is served barbecued on festive occasions. Below is an Australian version which is delicious with fruit chutney.

• SERVES 6 •

1 boned and butterflied leg of lamb, medium sized

Marinade

½ cup olive oil
juice of 1 lemon
1 tablespoon white wine
1 tablespoon honey
2 cloves garlic, crushed
1 tablespoon chopped rosemary, stalks removed
1 tablespoon grated ginger
mint leaves for decoration

Combine all the marinade ingredients and pour over the lamb. Leave for 8 hours if possible.

Heat the barbecue and cook the lamb for 15 minutes per side. Allow to stand for 10 minutes until the juices have settled. Carve into slices and serve, surrounded with mint leaves.

ARNI COTOLETTA MI FETTA

Ask your butcher to trim lamb racks for individual portions and cut pockets for stuffing.

• SERVES 4 •

4 lamb racks
4 tablespoons dry fetta cheese
2 tablespoons plain yoghurt
2 tablespoons chopped shallots
1 teaspoon green peppercorns
salt and pepper

Sauce

1 medium onion, finely chopped
3 tablespoons olive oil
4 ripe tomatoes, peeled and chopped
1 cup mint
1 tablespoon wine vinegar
salt and pepper

Mix the fetta, yoghurt, shallots, green peppercorns and seasoning. Stuff the pockets with the mixture.

Place the prepared lamb in a shallow baking dish and bake in a preheated oven, 250°C, for 10 minutes. Then turn the oven to 180°C and bake for a further 15 minutes.

To make the sauce, fry the onion in olive oil until soft. Add the tomatoes and cook for 20 minutes. Transfer the mixture to a food processor, add mint, vinegar, salt and pepper, and blend until smooth. Strain through a sieve and discard the solids. Arrange the cooked lamb racks on a platter and surround with the tomato and mint sauce.

POULI ABILOFILA MI STAFILLIA

This dish is a treat when prepared with fresh vine leaves. However, preserved vine leaves are also very good and are usually available from Greek grocery stores.

• SERVES 2 •

2 spatchcocks
salt and pepper
200 g small seedless white grapes
4 tablespoons butter
4 large vine leaves
toothpicks
2 tablespoons lemon juice
additional grapes for decoration

Season the spatchcocks inside with salt and pepper and insert 1 tablespoon of butter and 10 grapes in each. Melt the remaining butter in a shallow saucepan and brown the spatchcocks on each side. Leave to cool until comfortable to handle. Wrap each bird in 2 vine leaves, using toothpicks to secure. Place the spatchcocks in a casserole, breast down, cover and cook in a preheated oven, 200°C, for about 30 minutes, or until tender.

Remove the spatchcocks from the casserole and keep them warm. Press the remaining grapes through a sieve and stir the resulting liquid into the pan juices in the casserole. Add the lemon juice and heat gently, without boiling. Assemble the spatchcocks on a platter and surround with grapes and the sauce.

LITHRINI PLAKI

There is a unique Greek flavour to this baked fish made with honey, ouzo, citrus juices and herbs.

• SERVES 6 •

6 small bream, scaled and gutted or 6 jewfish or schnapper fillets
3 tablespoons olive oil
350 g onions, thinly sliced
1 teaspoon honey
500 g tomatoes, peeled, seeded and chopped
4 garlic cloves, finely chopped
1 bay leaf, crushed
½ teaspoon thyme
1 tablespoon orange juice
1 tablespoon lemon juice
2 tablespoons ouzo
salt and pepper
100 g kalamata olives, stoned and roughly chopped
2 tablespoons capers
400 g fennel tops, finely chopped
1½ cups rice

Wash and dry the fish of your choice and arrange in a single layer in an oiled baking dish.

Heat the oil in a frying pan and fry the onions until transparent. Add the honey, tomatoes, garlic, bay leaf, thyme, orange and lemon juice, ouzo and pepper to taste. Simmer the sauce until thickened — about 8 minutes. Stir in the olives, capers and fennel and pour the mixture over the fish.

Preheat the oven to 180°C and bake the fish for about 30 minutes. As the capers and olives are quite salty, taste the sauce before adding salt. Serve with soft rice.

SPANAKI KE PKASSA PILAFFI

To this Greek national favourite, we have added leeks for extra flavour.

• SERVES 4–6 •

2 leeks, cleaned and sliced
1 bunch fresh spinach
4 tablespoons olive oil
200 g Arborio rice
2 tablespoons chopped continental parsley
grated rind of 1 lemon
salt and pepper
1 tablespoon kasseri cheese, grated
2 teaspoons lemon juice

In a saucepan fry the leeks in the olive oil until they are soft but not mushy. Add the wet spinach and cook until the spinach is soft. Add the rice, parsley and grated lemon rind, and season with salt and pepper. Add 400 ml water and stir. Cover and cook slowly for 15 minutes. Keep the lid on until the water has fully evaporated. Stir in lemon juice and grated cheese.

POTATIS ME ROZ-MARI SKORTHO KE YAOURTI

Rosemary and garlic give this dish a distinctive Greek flavour and make it a suitable accompaniment for lamb dishes. It is important to use only the finest quality virgin olive oil. If you would like the potatoes to have a crusty appearance, sprinkle some finely grated kasseri cheese on top before cooking.

• SERVES 4–6 •

1 clove garlic, crushed
2 tablespoons olive oil
2 tablespoons fresh rosemary leaves, chopped
3 tablespoons yoghurt
salt and pepper
6 medium-sized potatoes, peeled and thinly sliced

In a bowl, mix crushed garlic, olive oil, rosemary, yoghurt and salt and pepper. Toss the sliced potatoes in this mixture. In a shallow, ovenproof flan dish, assemble the potatoes in layers. Bake at 180°C for about 45 minutes, or until the potatoes are cooked.

MELITSANA FETTES

These purple vegetables are excellent when salted and squeezed to remove bitterness, fried in oil and baked with tomato and kasseri cheese.

• SERVES 4 •

2 medium-sized eggplants
6 tablespoons olive oil
2 large tomatoes
4 slices kasseri cheese
salt, pepper and oregano

Slice the eggplant, salt generously and leave to drain in a colander for 1 hour. Squeeze gently to remove the excess moisture, then pat dry with a paper towel. Fry the eggplant in olive oil until just golden. Peel the tomatoes and cut into thick slices. Assemble individual piles consisting of layers of fried eggplant, tomato and kasseri, with eggplant on top, in an ovenproof dish. Sprinkle with oregano, salt and pepper. Drizzle a little olive oil on top and bake in a preheated oven (250°C) for 15 minutes.

REMISTA THIAFORA

Basil has always been of symbolic importance in Greek life: in ancient times it was used in the rites associated with love and death. The flavour of basil permeates these stuffed vegetables which make a delicious appetizer or accompaniment to meat or fish.

• SERVES 8 •

8 medium potatoes
8 medium tomatoes
8 zucchinis
grated kasseri cheese

Stuffing

1½ cups fresh basil leaves
2 tablespoons pine nuts
½ cup olive oil
1 clove garlic, crushed
1 teaspoon salt
pepper to flavour
chilli flakes
1 cup cooked rice
1 cup crumbed fetta cheese

Combine all the ingredients for the stuffing in a food processor, except the rice and fetta cheese. Blend until the mixture is a smooth paste. Place in a bowl and add the cheese and rice.

Bake the potatoes whole in the oven until cooked (about 40 minutes). Carefully scoop out the centre. Blanch and peel the tomatoes; remove the seeds and centres. Scoop out the centre of the zucchinis. Fill the vegetables with the stuffing.

Place on a baking dish, sprinkle with grated kasseri cheese and bake in a hot oven (200°C) for 15 minutes.

KEKI LEMONI

This easy-to-make cake contains favourite Greek ingredients: semolina, almonds and lemons.

• SERVES 8 •

2 lemons
juice of 1 lemon
5 medium-sized eggs
200 g sugar
100 g ground blanched almonds
50 g fine semolina flour

Line a round cake tin, 22 cm in diameter, with baking parchment.

Boil the lemons in water for 1 hour. When cool, cut into quarters and remove the seeds before blending to a pulp. Add the lemon juice to the pulp and mix well. Separate the eggs. Beat the egg yolks with 150 g of the sugar on high speed until the mixture is pale and the sugar is practically dissolved. Gently fold in the almonds and semolina, then add the lemon pulp and mix gently but thoroughly. Beat the egg whites until fairly stiff, then add 50 g of sugar and beat for a few more seconds. Gently fold the whites into the egg yolk mixture. When well incorporated, pour into the baking tin and bake in the oven at 180°C for 45 minutes. When cooked, turn the cake on to a cake rack and dust the top with icing sugar.

VASILOPITA

At New Year a special bread is baked. It is a yeast bread, fragrant with aromas of orange rind and spices, and decorated with blanched almonds and the numbers of the New Year.

• SERVES 6 •

15 g fresh yeast or 3 teaspoons dry yeast
¼ cup lukewarm milk
70 g butter, melted
2 beaten eggs
80 g sugar
1 tablespoon grated orange rind
½ teaspoon ground cinnamon
¼ teaspoon ground nutmeg
350 g unbleached plain flour
pinch of salt
1 beaten egg for glazing
blanched almonds for decoration

Dissolve the yeast in lukewarm milk and leave aside until it becomes frothy. Mix the butter, eggs, sugar, orange rind and spices. Sift flour and salt into a large bowl. Form a well in the centre and add all the other ingredients. Knead the dough well. Brush with melted butter, place the kneaded dough in the bowl, cover and allow to stand in a warm place until it has doubled in size. Shape into a round form and place on a well-buttered baking tray. Cover, and again allow it to double in size. Brush with the beaten egg and, with the almonds, form the numbers of the New Year on top. Bake in oven at 200°C for approximately 45 minutes.

BAKLAVA

Baklava consists of layers of light golden pastry with a filling of sugar, nuts and cinnamon, soaked in a rich honey-lemon syrup. It is the perfect accompaniment to strong Greek coffee.

• SERVES 6 •

Pastry

½ cup almonds, finely chopped
½ cup pistachio nuts, finely chopped
½ cup caster sugar
1 teaspoon cinnamon
1 teaspoon nutmeg
250 g filo
100 g melted butter

Syrup

1 cup sugar
¼ cup water
¼ cup lemon juice
finely grated rind of 1 lemon
finely grated rind of 1 orange
3 whole cloves
1 cinnamon stick
½ cup honey

First, make the syrup. Bring to the boil the sugar, water, lemon juice, citrus rinds and all the spices. Cook until the sugar dissolves and the mixture thickens. Discard the spices and add the honey. Cool the syrup.

To make the pastry, combine nuts, sugar, cinnamon and nutmeg. Brush a 20 × 10 cm baking tray with butter. Layer 5 sheets of filo, one on top of the other, brushing each layer with melted butter. Sprinkle one-third of the nut mixture over the filo. Repeat this procedure twice, ending with filo pastry.

Bake in the oven at 180°C for 45 minutes until brown. While hot, cut into squares with a sharp knife right down to the base. Pour the cooled syrup over the hot baklava. Allow to stand overnight before serving.

Spanish

SINCE 110 BC invading countries have left their influence on Spanish food. At that time the Phoenicians brought saffron and vines. The Celts brought pigs across the Pyrenees; consequently, ham and pork sausages feature strongly in the Basque diet. The Romans brought olives and the Arabs brought short grain rice, the basis of paella, together with almonds, citrus fruit, quinces, eggplant, spinach, cumin and sugar cane, and they also introduced sweet desserts.

In the sixteenth and seventeenth centuries the direction of this traffic was reversed. Spain was now the most powerful nation, ruling the Americas and half of Europe. To seek out new spices, Spanish explorers sailed the globe. They found them, and a new cuisine was born in Europe. Spain overran the Aztec and Mayan empires and brought back corn, peppers, beans, tomatoes, avocado, papaya, pumpkin, zucchini, guava, vanilla, chocolate, potatoes, sweet potatoes, and pecan and pine nuts. Spain became the leading and most fashionable culinary influence in Europe at that time.

The Spanish connection with Australia is said to have begun in 1595 when four Spanish ships sailed to the South Pacific from Peru to investigate an unknown continent. Carved on a rock face, overlooking the ocean at North Bondi, are two galleons and an inscription of ten letters:

believed to mean 'We in the Santa Barbara and Santa Ysabel conquered "W" from point to point. By the sign of the cross, signed by Lopez de Vega.'

In 1606 Luis Vaez de Torres, seeking Terra Australis, navigated the passage, now called Torres Strait, between Cape York and New Guinea. Later, in 1793, Alejandro Malaspiña visited the Spanish colonies in the South Seas and, on arriving at Port Jackson, reported to his government that the British had taken possession of this land.

John Macarthur forged another link with Spain and contributed significantly to Australian industry when, in 1790, he brought the first merino sheep here from Spain.

The Spaniards see themselves as a mixture of Don Quixote and his servant Sanchez, the characters created by Cervantes. Don Quixote is the idealist; Sanchez is the pragmatist. The combination of these two characteristics typifies the Spanish people.

In their enthusiasm to acclaim early Spanish explorers, Spanish locals sometimes claim connections with Australia that, alas, cannot always be proven. A Spanish explorer is said to have named the Olgas in the Northern Territory after a Spanish queen, but in fact they were discovered by one Ernest Giles in 1872 and named after Queen Olga of Wurtenburg in Germany who was a patron of science. Bendigo, in Victoria, is said to derive its name from Buena Diego, but researchers of Australian place names consider it was named after a shepherd called Bendigo. Nor was Dee Why named by a Spaniard, de Vega, but by James Meehan, probably as an abbreviation of the botanical name of a tree which he found growing in the area. The Barossa Valley, however, *was* named after a village in a wine-growing district of Spain.

Only a few isolated Spaniards arrived last century. Bishop Salvado established a Benedictine monastery at New Norcia, north of Perth, and it became, and has remained, a centre for music and wine-growing. In 1860, Jose Parer, a forebear of Damien Parer, the famous war photographer, opened the first Spanish restaurant in Melbourne.

Some Spaniards came to Australia during the Spanish Civil War in the late 1930s, but they arrived only in appreciable numbers in the 1950s. Initially, they came in Italian ships; the first Spanish ship arrived in 1960. The Spanish Government paid the fares of single people under thirty. The young men were the first to come, to work as cane-cutters in Queensland and on the tomato farms in Mildura. They were followed by the women in what was called 'The Bride Boat'.

The largest Spanish community is in Sydney, followed by Melbourne and Brisbane, with smaller numbers living in Western Australia, the Australian Capital Territory and Cairns, the centre for the earlier cane-cutters. The communities are fairly closely knit and also enthusiastic about their native food, customs and life which they have adapted in their own fashion. Their clubs are the hub of many social activities.

In Sydney the headquarters are in Liverpool Street where the Spanish Club owns its own premises with a coffee shop, restaurant, child-care centre, language classes and other educational pursuits. At Christmas time the club imports for its members champagne, cider and sherries from the homeland. Nearby are Spanish food shops where the floors are stacked with wicker-covered wine flagons and casks of olive oil. Dried salted cod, bacalao, hangs from the rafters. Restaurants, some featuring flamenco dancing, all serve great traditional dishes and Spanish wines. These robust, full flavoured wines go better with Spanish food than the more subtle and delicate French and German wines.

The Spanish custom of serving tapas is observed in these restaurants and also in some fashionable eateries in Paddington. Tapas are often eaten at lunchtime or shared with friends over drinks and conversation. The range of tapas is extensive, the most popular being empanadas, tortillas, eggs in mayonnaise and various preparations of sardines.

In summer the Spanish often hold barbecue picnics at many of the foreshore parks (Bronte beachside park is very popular). At these gatherings, the most famous of wine coolers, sangria, is served to wash down grilled sardines and copious plates of paella.

Just as Liverpool Street is the Sydney centre of eating and social activity, so too is Johnson Street in Fitzroy, Melbourne. Here is the Spanish Club, Hogar Español, and here also we found restaurants and shops with all the foods and ingredients for a delicious Spanish meal.

Festivals, both religious and national, are celebrated at the clubs. Christmas is the most important family festival. A large festive meal — usually seafood — is eaten before going to Midnight Mass. The meal sometimes continues after church with sweets such as ice cream, turron (an almond and honey nougat of Arabian origin) or pomporones (biscuits made with marzipan). To wash this down, Spanish cider or sangria is served. Lunch on Christmas Day may be fish or roast turkey and dried ham called jamonserrano, available at most good delicatessens.

Epiphany, on 6 January, is Kings' Day when the three wise Kings brought their gifts to the Christ child. On this day, gifts are exchanged. The Spanish clubs throw a big party and distribute presents to the children. The special food on this day is rosca de reyes, a sweet bread baked in the shape of a ring and containing either a bean, ring, coin or trinket. It is said that the person who receives the gift will have good luck all year round. Another dish appropriate to this day is los reyes canelloni.

During the first two days of Easter, meat is not eaten and most Spanish people would not eat meat during the preceding week. But on Sunday, a typical meal might be a barbecue of Spanish sausages and lamb, followed by a burnt cream custard and cakes.

Among the secular holidays observed here, 12 October marks the discovery of America by Christopher Colombus. The Festival of San Fermin on 7 July celebrates the resistance to Napoleon's invasion of Spain. In Pamplona a large herd of bulls runs free in the streets and in the afternoon there are bullfights. Less spectacularly, but no less enthusiastically, people here meet at their clubs and cafes to dip their churros in hot chocolate and keep alive their heritage.

TORTILLA CON BONIATO Y CALABASA

Tortilla is the classic potato omelette. For this recipe we have substituted kumera and pumpkin for the potato to give it a rich, golden colour and piquant flavour. It makes a perfect first course or an ideal luncheon dish.

• SERVES 6 •

600 g kumera
600 g sweet orange pumpkin
2 onions
1 cup vegetable oil
6 eggs
salt and freshly ground pepper
½ teaspoon Spanish paprika

Peel and thinly slice the kumera and pumpkin. Finely chop the onions. Mix the vegetables together.

Heat the oil in a large frypan and fry the vegetables until they are nearly cooked. Drain all the oil from them.

In a large bowl, beat the eggs and add the drained and cooked vegetables. Mix together. Add salt, pepper and paprika to taste.

Brush a non-stick frypan with oil and heat. Add the egg and vegetable mixture and cook over a moderate heat until the eggs set. Cover the frypan with a plate, turn upside down and slide the uncooked side back into the frypan. Cook for a further few minutes until it feels firm but will slide around the bottom of the pan. Serve hot or cold, cut into wedges.

ENSALADA DE PATO Y PERAS

In this salad the combination of sweet pear and slightly bitter endive provides a delicious accompaniment to the smoked flavour of the duck breast. Smoked duck breasts are not easily obtained but this salad also works well with other delicate smoked meat.

• SERVES 4 •

2 smoked duck breasts, thinly sliced
200 g endive
2 medium-sized pears, thinly sliced
salt and pepper
2 tablespoons walnut oil
1 tablespoon wine vinegar

Arrange on a platter washed, dried and separated endive. Place the sliced duck breasts in the centre. Surround the duck with slices of pear. Sprinkle with salt and pepper. Mix together the walnut oil and vinegar, and distribute evenly over the salad.

ATUN ESCABECHADO

Marinated tuna is versatile. It can be sliced thinly and served on top of salad greens or on freshly buttered rye bread.

• SERVES 6–8 •

300 g single piece of tuna
2 tablespoons wine vinegar
1 tablespoon olive oil
1 tablespoon onion, finely chopped
1 tablespoon capers, finely chopped
2 tablespoons parsley, finely chopped
1 tablespoon brown sugar
2 teaspoons salt
1 teaspoon pepper, freshly ground

Make a paste with all the ingredients, except the tuna. Place the tuna on clear plastic wrap large enough to envelop the tuna. Cover one side with half the marinade; turn the tuna on to the other side and spread with the remaining marinade. Wrap tightly and leave in the refrigerator for about 18–24 hours. When ready, slice thinly and arrange on a plate.

HUEVOS A LA FLAMENCA

A tasty luncheon dish using the most familiar of all Spanish sausage, chorizo.

• SERVES 4 •

3 tablespoons olive oil
2 onions, chopped
2 cloves garlic, finely chopped
½ green pepper, finely chopped
½ red pepper, finely chopped
4 ripe tomatoes, peeled and chopped
200 g chorizo, sliced
1½ cups cooked green peas
4 eggs
1 tablespoon dry sherry
salt and pepper to taste

In a frypan, heat the oil and fry the onions, garlic and peppers. Stir in tomatoes, salt and pepper, and cook until the mixture thickens slightly. Add chorizo.

Grease 4 individual ovenproof soufflé dishes, or 1 medium-sized dish. Spoon in the peas, then the onion and tomato mixture. Break an egg into each, sprinkle with sherry and freshly ground pepper, and cover with alfoil. Bake in a moderate oven (180°C) for 15 minutes or until the eggs are just set.

CHORIZO CON PAN

The speciality of shepherds in the north of Spain is bread thickened with egg and oil, and flavoured with chorizo. It is quite delicious and very easy to make. Use country-style bread for this dish. Chorizo can be obtained from Spanish delicatessens.

• SERVES 6 •

6 slices of bread
2 tablespoons olive oil
100 g chorizo, thinly cut
2 cloves garlic, crushed
salt and pepper
1 teaspoon paprika
¼ teaspoon cumin
2 eggs

Put the bread in a dish and sprinkle with a little water, making sure it is slightly damp all over. Heat the oil in a frying pan and sauté the sliced chorizo and crushed garlic. Season the bread with salt, pepper, paprika and cumin, add to the pan and cook over a low heat, turning from time to time until it is slightly crisp but not brown.

Beat the eggs well with a whisk. Arrange the cooked bread and chorizo in an ovenproof dish, pour over the beaten eggs and cook in a moderate oven (180°C) for 30 minutes.

VEGETALES CON SALSA ROMESCO

Romesco is the most famous of all Catalonian sauces. The main problem in trying to create this sauce is to find an equivalent to the slightly hot pepper available in Spain. We have found that a purée of roasted red capsicums and powdered Spanish paprika gives an agreeable result. Although this sauce is traditionally served with fish or shellfish, we have used it here as an accompaniment to a variety of vegetables.

• SERVES 6 •

2 medium potatoes, preferably waxy, boiled and sliced
100 g green beans, steamed and cut in halves
2 medium zucchini, thinly sliced lengthwise
1 bunch asparagus, just cooked
1 Spanish onion, thinly sliced
1 red capsicum, roasted, skinned and sliced into thin strips
20 g pitted green Spanish olives, stuffed with pimento
few leaves of basil and parsley
1 hard-boiled egg, sliced

Sauce

½ cup red capsicum, roasted, skinned and puréed
2 medium tomatoes, peeled, seeded and chopped
2 slices French bread, lightly fried in olive oil
50 g blanched roasted almonds
¼ cup wine vinegar
2 cloves garlic
salt and pepper
1 teaspoon Spanish paprika
½ cup olive oil

Place all the ingredients for the sauce in a food processor and blend until it has the consistency of mayonnaise. Arrange the vegetables on a platter and spread the sauce on top or serve it separately. Decorate with olives, basil, parsley and egg.

MAYONNAISE

Spaniards say that the word mayonnaise comes from Mahon, the principal city of the island of Menorca, and that therefore mayonnaise is their creation. Home-made mayonnaise is simple to make and tastes much better than the commercial variety.

1 whole egg
1 egg yolk
½ teaspoon Dijon-style mustard
½ teaspoon salt
2 tablespoons lemon juice
1 cup olive oil

In a food processor or blender, place the whole egg, egg yolk, mustard, salt and lemon juice. Blend for a few seconds. Keep the motor running and, very gradually, add the oil until the mixture has thickened. Do not overbeat or the mayonnaise will curdle.

COCIDO CON POLLO

Every country has its one dish meal. In France it is the pot-au-feu; in Ireland, Irish stew. The Spanish have cocido. They are flexible dishes to which you can add a little more or a little less. Because of their simplicity they remain favourites.

• SERVES 6–8 •

1 cup chick peas
2 tablespoons olive oil
1 large rooster, cut into 8 pieces
½ cabbage, trimmed and coarsely chopped
4 small potatoes, peeled
4 small turnips, peeled
6 small carrots
4 small onions, peeled
150 g chorizo, thickly sliced
100 g cooked vermicelli

Soak the chick peas overnight in cold water. When ready to cook, drain and put them into a large saucepan, cover with water and bring to the boil. Reduce heat and cook, covered, for about 1 hour, or until tender.

Heat the olive oil in a large skillet and sauté the chicken pieces until lightly browned. Remove the chicken from the skillet and lightly fry all the vegetables. Put the chicken and vegetables into the saucepan with the chick peas and cook, covered, on a gentle heat for 1 hour, or until the chicken is cooked and the vegetables are tender. Five minutes before serving, add the chorizo and vermicelli.

To assemble, arrange the chicken around the edge of a warmed plate. Strain the chick peas and vermicelli and place them in the middle of the plate. Arrange the vegetables around them. Moisten the chicken with the reserved soup.

HUERTANA DI MURCIA

There are many varieties of paella, often served at a celebration or festival. To celebrate the festival of Romenia de la Fuensanta, the patron saint of Murcia, a Mediterranean province in the south-east of Spain, vegetable paella would be served as the vegetables in this region are tender and sweet.

• SERVES 6 •

6 tablespoons olive oil
2 large onions, chopped
2 cloves garlic, crushed
400 g short-grain rice
2 tomatoes, peeled, seeded and chopped
200 g green peppers, chopped
1 tablespoon chopped parsley
225 g small artichokes, cleaned and cut in wedges
225 g green beans, cut in 2 cm lengths
½ cup lima beans, soaked
½ cup green peas
3 carrots, thinly sliced
3 cups strong chicken stock
pinch saffron threads, soaked in 1 tablespoon hot water
freshly ground pepper
pinch cayenne pepper (optional)

Heat the oil in a large, heavy-bottomed frying pan. Fry the onions and garlic. Add rice and toss for a few minutes to coat in oil. Add all other ingredients, bring to the boil, lower to a medium heat and cook for 15 minutes, stirring occasionally, or until vegetables are tender. The liquid should be nearly evaporated and the rice should be slightly underdone. Turn off the heat, cover and leave undisturbed for 8–10 minutes until the rice has finished cooking and the liquid has evaporated. Season to taste.

MERLUZA A LA GALLEGA

This recipe comes from the north-western region of Galicia where fresh fish is plentiful. We have used salmon cutlets, but blue-eyed cod, jewfish, or any thick fleshy fish may be substituted.

• SERVES 6 •

6 Atlantic salmon cutlets
2 tablespoons olive oil
4 leeks, finely sliced
1 clove garlic, crushed
3 sprigs parsley, finely chopped
¼ teaspoon oregano
1 tablespoon chopped basil
1 bay leaf
½ teaspoon white wine vinegar
500 g red potatoes, peeled and sliced
salt and pepper to taste

Sauce

2 tablespoons butter
2 tablespoons chopped spring onions
½ cup white wine
1 red capsicum, skinned, roasted and blended to a paste
½ teaspoon Spanish paprika

In a shallow casserole, heat the olive oil and lightly fry the leeks, garlic, parsley, oregano, basil, bay leaf and the vinegar. Add the potatoes and sweat for 10 minutes until they are half cooked.

Place the salmon cutlets on top of the potato mixture, sprinkle with salt and pepper and cook for a further 10 minutes until the fish has turned a light pink.

Meanwhile, in a small saucepan heat the butter, add the spring onions and sauté for 1 minute. Add the white wine and simmer for 3 minutes. Add capsicum paste and paprika and cook for a further minute.

To serve, place the potato mixture on a platter, arrange the fish steaks on top and pour the sauce over before serving.

PATATAS CON ESPECIAS

Potatoes of any description are much favoured by the Spanish. They nearly always accompany a meal, sometimes served as tapas and often casserole style.

• SERVES 6 •

6 medium potatoes
4 tablespoons olive oil
2 tablespoons onion, finely chopped
2 garlic cloves, finely chopped
1 teaspoon Spanish paprika
½ teaspoon chopped, dried red chilli (seeded)
salt

Cover potatoes with salted water, bring to the boil and cook until tender but not mushy. Peel and cut into 5 mm slices.

Heat the oil in a large frypan. Sauté the finely chopped onion and garlic until soft. Add the potatoes and sauté all until lightly browned. Sprinkle the paprika, chilli and salt on top. Cook for 4–5 minutes, turning occasionally.

CREMA QUEMADA A LA CATALANA

Custard and puddings are very popular in Spain. Crema Catalana is a version of burnt cream custard which is claimed to be a Spanish innovation. This dessert is delicately scented with citrus peel and cinnamon. It is delicious served with fresh figs.

• SERVES 6 •

Custard

500 ml milk
120 g sugar
peel from 1 lemon
1 cinnamon stick
6 egg yolks
30 g cornflour

Caramel

150 g sugar
1 tablespoon water

In a saucepan, bring the milk, half the sugar, and the lemon peel and cinnamon to the boil. Cover and allow to infuse.

In a bowl, beat the egg yolks with the remaining sugar until pale, then fold in the sifted cornflour. Dilute this mixture with a few ladlefuls of the infused milk and whisk well.

Bring the milk to the boil again, pour in the egg mixture and cook the cream until it thickens, whisking all the time. When ready, remove the lemon peel and cinnamon. Pour into a serving dish.

To make the caramel, put the sugar into a small heavy saucepan and place over a moderate heat. Cook until the sugar turns a golden colour. Add the water and let the mixture bubble for a few seconds. Remove from the heat and trickle over the custard.

ROSCA DE REYES

Sweet bread, formed into a ring and decorated with candied fruit and nuts, is baked to celebrate the manifestation of Christ to the three Kings on 6 January. It is a day for giving and receiving gifts.

• SERVES 6 •

3 tablespoons lukewarm water
3 teaspoons dry yeast
350 g unbleached plain flour
¼ teaspoon salt
80 g butter
80 g sugar
3 tablespoons lukewarm milk
2 eggs, lightly beaten
2 tablespoons grated orange and lemon rind
1 tablespoon brandy
1 lightly beaten egg for glazing
crystallised citrus peel
crystallised red cherries, halved
10 whole blanched almonds
1 tablespoon pine nuts

Dissolve the yeast in lukewarm water and leave aside until it becomes frothy. Sift the flour and salt into a large bowl. Cream the butter and sugar until light and fluffy. Add the milk, citrus rind, eggs and brandy, and stir well. Make a well in the centre of the flour and pour in the yeast mixture. Add the butter, sugar, egg and milk mixture. Knead the dough until smooth and elastic. Oil the bowl and place the dough in the bowl. Cover with damp cloths and allow to stand in a draught-free place until it has doubled in size.

When the dough is ready, shape into a ring and place on a buttered baking tray. Place a jar in the middle of the ring to keep the shape. Leave it until it has again doubled in size. Brush with lightly beaten egg and sprinkle with crystallised fruit and nuts. Bake in a moderate oven, 180°C, for 35–40 minutes. Traditionally, a little gift — a trinket or a coin — is hidden in the cake.

PANELLETS

Panellets are delicious marzipan cakes, eaten in Catalonia on All Saints Day on 1 November when families visit cemeteries and remember their departed relatives.

• MAKES 20–24 •

200 g freshly ground almonds
75 g finely crushed stale cake crumbs
grated rind of 1 lemon
200 g sugar
2½ tablespoons cornflour
lightly beaten egg white
100 g pine nuts
55 g desiccated coconut

Line a baking tray with cooking parchment or grease and sprinkle with flour.

Mix together the almonds, cake crumbs and lemon rind. Gradually add the sugar, kneading well. Form the mixture into 20–24 balls, roll in cornflour and then in the beaten egg white. Finally, roll in pine nuts and coconut.

Place the balls on a baking tray. Bake for 15 minutes in a preheated oven at 230°C. Leave to cool before serving.

CHURROS

Churros are a fried batter made with water and milk. They are eaten at breakfast time, dipped in coffee or hot chocolate. It is also a custom in Spain to serve them with hot chocolate at the end of a long day. They will always be seen at Spanish festivals, frying in huge cauldrons of oil. They must be eaten immediately once cooked.

• MAKES 24 •

¼ litre water
¼ litre milk
pinch of salt
1 tablespoon oil
500 g flour
oil for frying
granulated sugar for dipping

Put water, milk, salt and 1 tablespoon of oil in a saucepan and place on the stove. When the mixture boils, remove from the heat and gradually add the flour, stirring all the time with a wooden spoon for approximately 5 minutes until the mixture becomes a smooth paste. Place the mixture in an icing bag with a fluted tube and press the paste out into strips or loops approximately 10 cm long. Heat the oil in a frying pan to a medium to hot temperature, fry the churros until golden brown on one side, then turn and fry to a golden brown on the other side. Drain on a paper towel, dip in sugar and serve warm.

CHOCOLATE

This drink is traditionally served at breakfast, tea time or on returning home from Mass, with churros, which are dunked in the chocolate.

• SERVES 4 •

4 cups milk
125 g unsweetened chocolate, broken into pieces
10 teaspoons sugar, more or less to taste

Mix together all the ingredients. Heat over a low flame, beating with a wire whisk until chocolate has melted. Bring to the boil, allow to bubble and remove from heat. Beat with a wire whisk until very frothy and serve immediately.

SANGRIA

Summers in Spain are long and hot, and it has long been a tradition to drink icy cold sangria, which is a red wine punch. This recipe is easy to prepare and the ingredients can be increased by any amount desired.

• MAKES 6 CUPS •

1 bottle red wine
2 tablespoons fresh orange juice
2 tablespoons Grand Marnier
2 tablespoons advocaat
1 tablespoon sugar
1 orange, cut into wedges
1 lemon, cut into wedges
apple, peach and nectarine wedges
1 cup soda water
ice cubes

Mix all the ingredients, except the soda water, in a large jug. Cover and refrigerate for several hours. Before serving, add the soda water and ice cubes.

Jewish

FOOD, like all features of a people's culture, is a reflection of their history — it doesn't just happen overnight, but evolves over time.

Jewish food reflects the history of a people without a homeland for two thousand years, scattered throughout the known world. Its uniqueness stems from their wanderings through many different countries, absorbing local flavours and adapting local products. It comes, too, from its association with religious and traditional festivals. Suffering and deprivation taught the Jewish people to make the most of whatever foods were available.

For many years potatoes were the staple diet of Eastern Europe so the Jewish housewife devised many ways to prepare them. One of the most popular traditional recipes today is the latke.

When the First Fleet arrived in Sydney on 26 January 1788, it carried sixteen Jewish convicts. Subsequently, more convicts and many free settlers of the Jewish faith arrived from England.

In their book, *Genesis*, Levi and Bergman record that as early as 8 April 1830 the *Sydney Gazette* reported a meeting of Jews for a Passover service. The *Monitor*, on 10 April of that same year, printed a letter describing the first communal Passover meal or seder. The letter signed by 'A Hebrew' ends 'We had plenty of Clice (Kleis), but alas no Coogle (Kugel)'.

Matzoh, the unleavened bread, was made in Sydney and in the 1830s Jewish prisoners on Norfolk Island were receiving matzoh. Supplies were also shipped from Sydney to the other colonies.

The *Illustrated Australian News* of 5 March 1887 carried a picture titled 'Making Passover Cakes'. (The original paper is held by the Mitchell Library in Sydney.)

In the first and second decades of the nineteenth century came Russian and Polish Jews, escaping the pogroms and enforced military service, and bringing with them their religious and culinary customs. The 1930s saw an influx of refugees from middle European countries already, or about to be, occupied by Hitler. In 1956, following the uprising in Hungary, many Hungarian Jews arrived here.

All these newcomers brought new additions to the Australian menu: borscht, torte, schnitzel and goulash.

The earlier arrivals in this century settled in the inner suburbs of Newtown, Redfern and Surry Hills in Sydney. Today, the Jewish population is centred mainly in the Eastern Suburbs and on the North Shore, with smaller numbers in the west and south of Sydney.

In Sydney, most of the Jewish food suppliers are located at Six Ways, Bondi. Here are restaurants, kosher butchers, cake shops and delicatessens, with a seemingly endless variety of foods which have been introduced to, and are now firmly part of, the Australian diet.

When Jewish immigrants first arrived in Melbourne, they settled around the ports and around the city centre, in Carlton and St Kilda. They then moved out to Elwood, Caulfield, Toorak and Kew. The famous Jewish shopping centres are in Carlisle and Acland Streets. Acland Street replicates the European custom of sitting in coffee shops and discussing important matters of state, while the quality of conversation is enhanced by delicious cakes and coffee. Carlisle Street is more down to earth and housewives shop there for kosher meat, bread, pickles and bagels.

Jewish people observe the religious laws of Kashrut — dietary laws which prohibit the consumption of certain foods, require ritual and humane killing of animals and forbid the mixing of meat and milk.

Because of these limitations Jewish cooks had to become skilled in preparing fish. They chopped and mixed together different sorts of fish — whatever was available in the places they found themselves — added spices and seasonings, and so created gefilte fish. This literally means 'stuffed'. The flesh was removed from the skin, prepared and put back inside the skin, and served as a whole fish. A more usual way today is to roll the mixture into small balls and cook them in fish stock.

Every country to which the Jewish people dispersed contributed something to their cuisine. From Russia came borscht, blintzes (very thin pancakes with a variety of fillings, most commonly, cheese), pickled red cabbage, black bread and fruit compotes. From Hungary came the paprika to flavour stews and meats, and from Germany came sweet and sour stews and kugel, or pudding. Spain and Portugal contributed spicy peppers and olives, and the custom of frying fish and other foods in oil. In Lithuania herrings were plentiful and many ways were devised by the Jewish people to make this lovely fish more interesting.

Food is an important part of family life. To the old dictum 'The family that prays together stays together', one could add 'The family that eats together meets together'. Every Sabbath and festival sees families coming together for traditional meals and each occasion has its characteristic dishes.

On the Sabbath, Jewish families usually congregate for Friday night dinner or Saturday lunch. A traditional meal might be chicken soup with lockshen (egg noodles) or kreplach (dumplings), then chopped liver or gefilte fish and roast chicken with salad or vegetables, followed by, perhaps, lockshen kugel (an egg noodle pudding) or fruit compote.

The table is decorated with a decanter of wine with which to make a blessing, plaited poppyseed loaves of bread called challah and, on Friday night, two lit candles over which the blessing is made by the female members of the house.

The Fourth Commandment forbids work on the Sabbath so cooking cannot be done on that day. Kindling a fire also requires effort — this law developed long before the advent of the automatic oven. To satisfy the Fourth Commandment, cholent was conceived. This dish is prepared on Friday, before Sabbath, and put on a very low fire or in a very slow oven to cook overnight.

The Jewish New Year is called Rosh Hashanah, the first day of the religious year. Sweet foods are served as symbols of the desire for a sweet new year. These include honey cake, carrot tzimmes and apple slices dipped in honey.

Succot is the festival of the wheat harvest.

It also commemorates the forty years wandering in the wilderness after the deliverance of the Israelites from Egypt. During the festival, meals are taken in a temporary structure in the garden. This is called a succah, the roof of which is made from palm leaves, partially open to the sky. A variety of fruit is hung from the branches and, customarily, strudel filled with fruit and nuts is served.

Chanuka, the Festival of Lights, commemorates the rededication of the Temple of Jerusalem in 165 BC, after it had been reclaimed by the victorious Maccabees. Oil to kindle the candelabrum, the menorah, was sufficient for one day only but, miraculously, it lasted for eight days. So for eight days candles are lit on a menorah, one on the first day, two on the second day, and so on.

Symbolic of the oil are fried pancakes, the batter for which can be made of potato or flour.

Purim is a gay and happy festival, based on the 'Book of Esther' in the Bible, and celebrated in February or March. Two and a half thousand years ago Esther, a beautiful Jewish woman, became Queen of Persia and saved her people from destruction, planned by Haman, the King's chief minister. A commandment of this book is to observe Purim as 'a day of feasting and gladness and sending portions to one another and gifts to the poor'.

A favourite Purim delicacy is hamantaschen or Haman pockets, three-cornered pastries that are filled with poppyseeds, raisins or plum jam. Another Purim dish is kreplach, triangular pieces of dough filled with minced meat and served in a soup.

Passover celebrates the flight of the Israelites from Egypt and slavery. In their haste to depart, the dough they were making for bread did not have time to rise. This is commemorated during the festival by not eating foods which contain leavening agents. Bread is replaced with an unleavened bread called matzoh or 'the bread of affliction'.

YOICH

For Jewish people, the panacea for all ills is a golden, fragrant chicken soup. There are innumerable recipes for this. The secret to a tasty and rich flavour is to use a large boiling fowl. The slow, prolonged cooking fills the whole house with delicious smells.

• SERVES 6 •

2.5 kg boiling fowl
250 g carrots, peeled and chopped
250 g onions, chopped
1 small parsnip, chopped
1 stick celery, chopped
1 tablespoon whole peppercorns
2 tablespoons salt
bouquet garni (parsley, bay leaves, thyme)

Place the chicken in a large pot and cover with water. Bring to the boil and skim the top. Cover and allow to simmer for 1 hour. Add the carrots, onions, parsnip, celery, bouquet garni and seasoning. Simmer for a further hour. Leave the soup to cool in the refrigerator overnight. By the next day the fat will have formed into a hard crust. Remove the fat and the soup is ready for reheating and serving with any of the traditional accompaniments, such as knaidlach (matzoh balls), lockshen (noodles) or kreplach (filled dumplings).

KREPLACH

Kreplach is dough, filled with ground meat, which is boiled or fried, and served in soup or as a side dish.

• SERVES 6 •

1 cup flour
1 egg
salt to taste
2 tablespoons water
oil for frying

Filling

1 cup ground meat
1 tablespoon grated onion
salt and pepper to taste

Combine flour, egg, salt and water. Knead, then roll out thinly on a floured board. Cut into 6 cm squares.

In a bowl, combine ground meat, onion, salt and pepper. Mix well. Put a dessertspoon of mixture on each square of dough. Form into triangles, press edges together and boil or fry in shallow oil until triangles fill out.

Knaidlach

Knaidlach are fluffy balls, made from matzoh meal, which are served in chicken soup. They are the traditional start to the Passover meal. Making knaidlach is an art and different methods, handed down from generation to generation, are guarded with secrecy and rivalry.

• MAKES 8 BALLS •

1 cup matzoh meal
2 tablespoons oil
2 tablespoons cold water
2 eggs, beaten with fork
½ teaspoon salt
½ teaspoon pepper

Combine all ingredients except matzoh meal. Add matzoh meal gradually, stirring into other ingredients. Refrigerate for 20 minutes in a covered bowl. Form into balls and drop into boiling salted water to which you can add a chicken stock cube. The pot in which they are cooked should be large to allow for expansion. Cook for 30 minutes on a low heat. Take out with a slatted spoon. Add to chicken soup.

Gehackte Leber

A poor man's pâté de foie gras has been a favourite appetizer with Jewish people for several hundreds of years. It is a mixture of slowly cooked onions, fried chicken livers and hard-boiled eggs, chopped together. Recipes for this dish vary among the different Jewish communities. To obtain the best results only the freshest chicken livers should be used, and dedicated cooks always use chicken fat for frying, although cholesterol watchers may prefer to use margarine.

• SERVES 6 •

250 g chicken livers
150 g onions, chopped
3 tablespoons chicken fat or margarine
6 hard-boiled eggs
salt and pepper

Fry the onions in chicken fat until they have softened. Add the whole chicken livers and fry on a medium heat for 15 minutes. Put aside. When cool, chop all the ingredients finely by hand. Add salt and pepper to taste. (Blending them in a food processor is unsatisfactory because the mixture becomes too smooth.)

GEFILTE FISCH

This is one of those dishes that is prominent on many Jewish festive occasions. There are many versions of gefilte fish, depending on the kind of fish that can be obtained by the particular community. In Australia, we have a great variety of fish so the local recipes are much more imaginative in their use of fish. Although the choice of fish below is not obligatory, it is better to select fish that have contrasting flavours, textures and colour. The dish can be presented in dumpling form, or the minced fish can be encased in the skin of the fish.

• SERVES 6 •

250 g carp (whole)
250 g blue-eyed cod (without skin)
150 g onions, sliced
4 carrots, sliced
1 slice challah (white bread)
2 egg yolks
1 tablespoon parsley
salt and pepper
2 egg whites

Prepare fish stock with the bones and offcuts of the fish, sliced onion and carrots.

Carefully remove the skin from the carp, keeping it as intact as possible. Mince the fish. Soak the bread in water and squeeze out all the moisture. Mix thoroughly the minced fish, the egg yolks, the bread and the seasonings. Beat the egg whites until firm and gently fold through the above mixture.

Spread the fish skin flat, place the mixture on top and form into a log. The leftover mixture can be used to make oval-shaped dumplings.

Strain the fish stock and bring to the boil. Place the fish log and the dumplings very gently into the simmering stock and cook for about 45 minutes. When cooked, remove from the stock and arrange on a platter. Save the remaining stock, which will turn into jelly when cold. Serve the fish cold, accompanied by fish jelly and horseradish relish.

CHOLENT

A traditional pot roast served on the Sabbath. An observant religious household does not cook on Friday night and Saturday. In the past, cholent was cooked on an open fire on Friday afternoon and left warming on the remaining embers for the Sabbath lunch. It is an ancient dish that has travelled with Jewish people wherever they have gone. Naturally it has been adapted to suit local conditions so there are many different recipes for cholent. The best smoked brisket of beef can be obtained from kosher butchers and gives a nice fragrance.

• SERVES 6 •

100 g onions, chopped
1 tablespoon oil
200 g boiling beef
200 g smoked brisket of beef
200 g haricot beans
150 g whole barley
1 tablespoon paprika
salt and pepper
200 g potatoes, peeled and coarsely chopped

Fry the onions in the oil until soft. Add the two kinds of beef and seal them on all sides. Put the beans, barley and seasoning into the pot and cover it all with water. Bring to the boil. Reduce the heat, cover and cook slowly until the beans and barley are still firm but nearly cooked. Add the peeled potatoes and simmer until the potatoes are cooked.

To serve, slice the beef and place it on a bed of beans and barley. Arrange the potatoes around the beef.

HOLISHKES

This is a popular Eastern European dish which found its way into Jewish cuisine. The reason for the popularity of cabbage rolls is that they can be cooked ahead and are still delicious when reheated.

• SERVES 6 •

12 cabbage leaves
250 g lean minced meat
100 g rice
2 tablespoons chopped parsley
1 tablespoon chopped dill
1 teaspoon paprika
salt and pepper
1 tablespoon olive oil or vegetable oil
2 onions, chopped
125 g tomato paste
juice of 1 lemon

Scald the cabbage leaves with boiling water to soften them. Leave to one side. Combine the meat, rice, parsley, dill and seasoning. Place a heaped spoonful of the mixture at the stem of each cabbage leaf, turn in the sides and roll into neat packages.

Heat the oil in a large saucepan and fry the onions until soft. Add tomato paste and cook for a few seconds. Remove two-thirds of this mixture from the saucepan and set aside. Place a layer of cabbage rolls on top of the mixture in the saucepan. Spread some of the tomato paste and onion mixture on top and continue in the same way, finishing with the tomato paste. Cover with water and lemon juice, bring to the boil and allow to cook slowly for about 1 hour.

FLEISH MIT FLOHMEN TZIMMES

As with all other traditional tzimmes dishes, this combines sweet and sour flavours.

• SERVES 6 •

500 g brisket of beef
50 g onions
1 tablespoon oil
150 g prunes, strained
juice of 1 lemon
1 tablespoon honey
salt and pepper
1 litre beef stock
6 potatoes, steamed

Gently brown the onions and beef in the oil for 15 minutes. Add the prunes, lemon juice, honey and seasoning, and cover with beef stock. Bring to the boil. Cover, and simmer slowly until half the liquid has evaporated and the meat is tender.

Serve sliced, surrounded by the cooked prunes and accompanied by the potatoes.

HELZEL

This is made from skin taken from the neck of a chicken, goose, turkey or duck, which is then stuffed and baked. The ingredients for the stuffing may vary slightly. Turkish Jews add chopped walnuts; Oriental Jews add saffron and cinnamon, and ground meat instead of breadcrumbs. Helzel is served with roasted chicken or meat.

• SERVES 2–4 •

1 skin of the chicken neck
2 tablespoons matzoh meal or breadcrumbs
2 tablespoons flour
6 tablespoons chopped onion
salt and freshly ground pepper
2 tablespoons melted chicken fat or margarine

Mix all ingredients for the stuffing and loosely fill the skin of the neck. Sew up both ends. Roast next to meat or chicken, basting with pan juices from time to time. Cook for approximately 60–80 minutes. When ready, remove, carve and serve with gravy.

CHRAIN

Horseradish is a bitter herb, traditionally eaten at Passover to symbolise the bitter years spent in exile. Here, it is combined with beetroot to make a delicious salad.

• SERVES 6 •

500 g beetroot
100 g Spanish onions
3 tablespoons horseradish relish
2 tablespoons wine vinegar
salt and pepper

Wrap the beetroot in baking foil and bake in the oven at 180°C for half an hour. When the beetroot are cool, peel and slice them. Cut the onions into thin slices. Mix the horseradish relish with the vinegar, salt and pepper, and combine with the beetroot and onion. Leave the salad in the refrigerator for at least 2 hours before serving to allow the horseradish dressing to permeate the beetroot.

LATKES

Latkes are grated potato pancakes, delicious served with apple sauce or sour cream or, even better, both. They are regarded as a Chanuka treat. The oil in which they are cooked is a reminder of the miracle of Chanuka when a flask of oil burned for eight days instead of one and the Temple of Jerusalem was rededicated to the victorious Maccabees in 165 BC.

• SERVES 4–6 •

6 large potatoes
1 large onion
2 eggs, beaten
50 g flour
1 teaspoon salt
225 ml peanut oil

Coarsely grate the potatoes and press through a colander until all the water has been removed. It is important to remove as much moisture as possible for a successful latke. Grate the onion and add to the potato. Stir in eggs, flour and salt.

Heat the oil in a frying pan until it is very hot, then lower the heat. Add the mixture, one tablespoon at a time, to the oil. When the latkes are golden brown and the edges are crisp, turn them over and brown the other side. Serve immediately.

MEREN TZIMMES

Sweetened carrots, called tzimmes, are traditionally served on the night of Rosh Hashanah (New Year). The Yiddish word for carrots is meren, which also means 'increase'. This dish symbolises our desire for our virtues to surpass our shortcomings.

• SERVES 4 •

6 carrots
½ cup honey
1 tablespoon butter or margarine
equal quantities of water and orange juice to cover

Slice the carrots into very fine strips and place in a shallow saucepan with the honey and butter. Cover with orange juice and water and cook rapidly until most of the liquid evaporates and the carrots are cooked but not mushy.

HAMANTASCHEN

Hamantaschen are traditionally eaten at the Purim festival in memory of Queen Esther, a beautiful Jewish woman who became the Queen of Persia around 500 BC and saved her people from destruction planned by Haman, the King's chief minister. The name probably alludes to the three-pointed hats worn by Haman. These three-cornered pastries can be filled with a variety of delicious things: poppyseeds, dried fruit or prunes.

• MAKES 12–14 •

Pastry

250 g flour
2 tablespoons baking powder
2 eggs
6 tablespoons oil
grated rind of 1 lemon
100 g sugar

Filling

250 g stoned prunes
125 ml strong tea
4 tablespoons honey
1 tablespoon lemon juice

To make the pastry, sift flour and baking powder, then add well-beaten eggs, oil, lemon rind and sugar. Form into a pliable dough and roll out thinly. Cut into rounds.

To make the filling, cook the prunes in the tea until they are soft and half the liquid has evaporated. Mix in the honey and lemon juice. Blend the mixture in a food processor.

To assemble, place a spoonful of filling on each round and press the edges together to form a triangle. Bake in a moderate oven (180–200°C) for about 25 minutes.

STRUDEL

Succot, the Festival of Tabernacles, is the Jewish autumn festival, traditionally to celebrate the harvest. It is a joyous time which lasts for nine days in September/October. A booth, decorated with palm fronds, fruits and flowers, is erected outside the house and observant Jews eat all their meals there during the festival. The four plants traditionally associated with this festival are citron, palm, myrtle and willow. Dishes prepared with nuts, dried fruit and fresh fruit are popular at this time.

• SERVES 6 •

½ cup raisins
1 tablespoon sweet kosher red wine
3 cups apples, peeled and roughly cut
3 tablespoons sugar
½ cup melted unsalted butter
½ cup walnut pieces
6 sheets of filo pastry
½ cup ground walnuts
cinnamon
icing sugar for garnish

Scald the raisins with hot water and drain them well on a paper towel. Mix the wine and the raisins together and allow to stand for 1 hour.

In a shallow saucepan, gently fry the apples and sugar in 1 tablespoon of the melted butter until the apples have softened slightly and a little of the moisture has evaporated. Leave aside to cool. Add walnut pieces.

With a brush, butter one sheet of filo pastry, sprinkle with ground walnuts and cover with another sheet of filo. Again, butter and sprinkle with ground walnuts. Spread one-third of the fruit and walnut mixture on top of the prepared filo pastry. Fold the ends over first, then roll the pastry to form a log. Repeat this with the rest of the filo and fruit mixture to make three logs.

Place the strudels on a buttered baking tray, brush the tops with melted butter and sprinkle them with sugar and cinnamon. Bake in a preheated oven at 200°C for 20–30 minutes until crisp and golden.

To serve, cut each strudel in half and dust with icing sugar.

LOCKSHEN KUGEL

This is a traditional Jewish dessert made from fruit, noodles and custard. The word 'lockshen' is Yiddish for noodles. This dessert provides a nice balance for a Sabbath meal and is delicious served with freshly stewed fruit.

• SERVES 6–8 •

250 g egg noodles (cooked and drained)
¼ cup melted butter
70 g diced candied fruits (soak in rum for a few hours)
50 g sultanas
½ litre milk
150 g sugar
4 eggs, beaten
½ teaspoon cinnamon

Put the cooked noodles in to a large bowl and add the melted butter, fruit and milk. Mix together. Combine the sugar and the beaten eggs, and add to the noodle mixture. Pour into a greased 25 cm flan dish, sprinkle with cinnamon and bake in a moderate oven (150°C) for 40 minutes, or until it feels firm.

MATZOH BRIE

There are innumerable versions of these matzoh pancakes. They can be made sweet or savoury, as one large pancake or as small ones. This variation comprises a number of small sweet pancakes flavoured with cinnamon and raisins.

• SERVES 4 •

4 matzohs, crushed
¼ cup boiling water
3 eggs, separated
1 tablespoon raisins, chopped
3 tablespoons clarified butter
1 tablespoon caster sugar
1 teaspoon cinnamon

Put the matzoh into a bowl and dampen with the boiling water. Immediately remove all the moisture from the matzoh. Beat the egg yolks in a bowl and stir in the dampened matzoh. Beat the egg whites until they are stiff. Fold the egg whites and the raisins into the matzoh and egg yolk mixture.

Heat the butter in a frying pan. Drop tablespoons of the mixture into the hot butter and fry on both sides until lightly browned. Serve sprinkled with sugar and cinnamon.

Middle Eastern

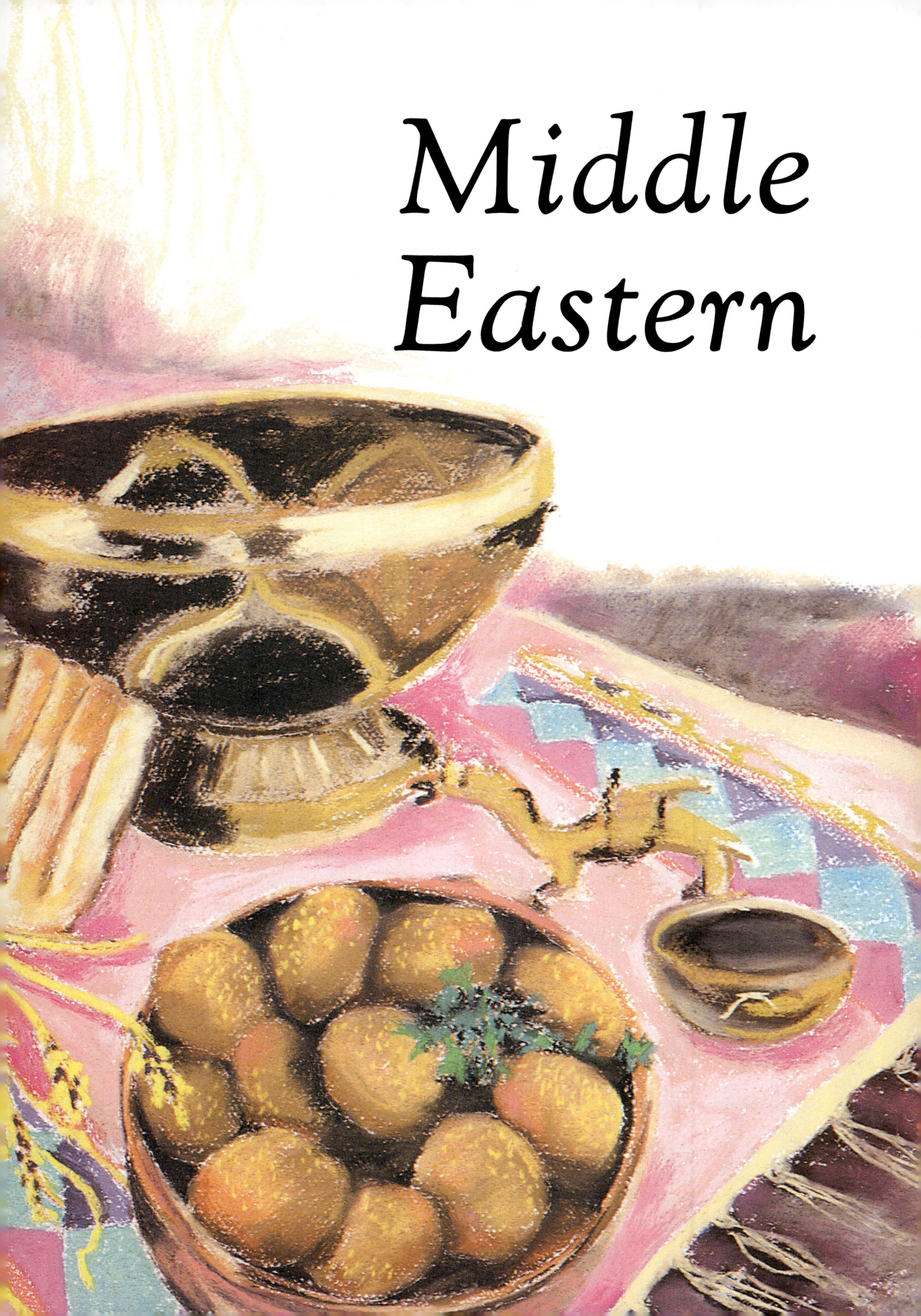

THE term 'Middle East' covers a diversity of lands stretching from Egypt in the west to Afghanistan in the east. Their language is in most part Arabic, their religion mostly Islamic, with some communities of Christians and Jews.

The countries whose stories we chose to explore were Lebanon, Turkey, Egypt, Iran and Israel. We used the same criteria we applied in choosing the chapters of this book.

LEBANESE

Lebanese migration to Australia has been in three phases: first from 1810 to 1914 when the opening of the Suez Canal meant more imports and a decline in traditional industries. Under Ottoman supremacy, Christians were persecuted and many fled to other countries. These early immigrants to Australia found it hard to get work and often became hawkers in country areas. When they had enough capital, they set up business in shopkeeping, manufacturing and wholesale warehousing and supplied the hawkers. There is today a sizeable Lebanese population in Dubbo and Cobar in New South Wales, but many who prospered have moved from country towns to be with their children who go to school in the city. In Sydney, they moved from Redfern to the eastern suburbs of Randwick, Kingsford, Maroubra and Coogee. In Victoria, while the males were hawkers in the country, their families remained in the inner city. With growing affluence, they moved to suburbs such as St Kilda and Kew.

Lebanese immigrants continued to arrive after World War II. Then from 1975 came the third wave because of the internecine strife in Lebanon. With this wave there was a marked increase in the number of Muslims. These later arrivals live in Sydney suburbs such as Marrickville, Arncliffe and Canterbury and, in Melbourne, in Brunswick, Coburg and Northcote.

The family unit is important and has figured in chain migration and sponsorship. Village associations, based on kinship and village ties, provide support for fellow villagers.

TURKISH

Most Turks came to Australia in the 1960s after an agreement between the two governments. They were largely unskilled workers who engaged in factory work and lived near the factory sites. Some went to rural areas, such as Shepparton, to work as tomato growers or pickers. There, the Turkish Cultural Group was founded; others were then established in Mildura and Red Cliffs. The Federation of Democratic Associations based in Sydney has ties with a number of worker organisations and unions.

There are now many cultural, educational and welfare associations: in Melbourne they are to be found in Brunswick, Mentone and Port Melbourne; in Sydney, in Redfern, Auburn and St Marys. Auburn, for example, is full of Turkish shops and restaurants.

Turkish Australians often present their folklore, especially folk dancing, for the edification of the general public and to reinforce their own ethnicity. Their staple diet has remained the same as it was in Turkey. For breakfast, it is customary to eat cheese, olives, tomatoes, marmalade and bread, and to drink lots of sweet black tea. Turkish coffee, strong, thick and sweet, is reserved for the end of lunch and dinner when it can be savoured slowly. Popular dishes enjoyed by Turkish families are pilau, a rice dish; shish kebab, pieces of meat grilled on a skewer; turlu, a mixture of vegetables and meat; taze fasulye, fresh green beans cooked with onions, tomatoes and olive oil, an important ingredient in Turkish cooking, and fasulye, dried beans.

In Sydney Road, Brunswick, Lebanese and Turkish shops sell a profusion of Middle Eastern ingredients: halal meat, beans, grains, unusual herbs, spices, and a marinated cheese, haloumi. The bakery sells all sorts of flat breads and pastries. The same foods can be easily found wherever there is a concentration of Muslim people.

EGYPTIAN

The early Egyptian immigrants to Australia in the 1960s were Christian. Under Nasser's regime, businesses were nationalised and the Islamic influence was intensified. Many of the Coptic minority no longer felt secure and emigrated to Australia.

In Sydney, they settled in Marrickville and there built the first Coptic Church. There are now at least five such churches in Sydney, three in Melbourne and one in Adelaide. The church is the heart of religious, social and educational activity. The clergy are the political and communal leaders.

Muslim Egyptians are considerably fewer in number. Most live in Sydney and Melbourne with a handful in other states. They are associated with other Muslim ethnic communities through the Australian Federation of Islamic Councils.

Browsing through a church market in Balmain, Sydney, we came upon a food stall manned by an Egyptian family. They were selling lamb on skewers, stuffed capsicum and zucchini, meat wrapped in vine leaves, brown beans and tahini dip.

IRANIAN

Iranians, formerly and perhaps more romantically, Persians, number only a few thousand in Australia. They are predominantly Muslims, but some are Bahais and Christians who came after the 1979 revolution which overthrew the Shah and are more western in their culture. In Sydney, they live in the western suburbs of Fairfield, Ryde, Auburn and Liverpool. Muslims attend their local mosque. The Iranian Anglican Church holds a monthly Persian service in the city for Iranian Christians.

The native language is Persian though Arabic letters are used in writing, which is from right to left.

ISRAELI

In the first decade of this century, some Jewish emigrants came from Israel, then called Palestine and under Turkish control. Most of these families settled in Perth, perhaps because it was the nearest port after a long voyage, and others followed in a chain migration. Because they had only their Hebrew learning, like the Lebanese, many Jewish men also became hawkers to country towns and some settled in those towns as shopkeepers. Some who had been on the land at home became farmers.

The foods that the wives cooked in their old country and then in the new were a combination of those traditional recipes we have mentioned in the Jewish section and others common to their geographical place in the Middle East. These were recipes using aubergine, marrow stuffed with minced meat and rice, and cabbage rolls or prakes which are similar to dolmades. Sesame seeds were used in cooking and halva was a popular sweet. Sephardic Jews whose ancestors had, after their expulsion from Spain in 1492, settled in Middle Eastern countries, came centuries later to Israel and then to Australia and brought with them the ubiquitous felafel, or chick pea croquettes, with hummus and tahina.

Since the Six Day War and subsequent tensions in the Middle East, some few thousand Israelis have come to Australia and have popularised Israeli foods such as fruit soups, carrot pudding and cake, chicken cooked with fruit, turkey stuffed with dried fruits and the use of sesame with poultry and sweets. Israeli-style restaurants are to be found in Bondi and East Sydney and in the Melbourne suburbs of Caulfield and Elsternwick. Ingredients for cooking are sold in shops there also.

In the seventh century, the Arabs invaded and established an Islamic empire across Asia and North Africa. Their own diet, like their Bedouin habits, was spartan, but through the centuries gave way to the indulgent foods of the more hedonistic countries they occupied. Rice spread as a crop as far as Spain. Transport and trade on a vast scale brought olive oil, dates, coffee, spices and even dried fish from Russia.

The Golden Age of the Arabic empire was superseded by the Ottoman empire in the fourteenth century. Its sovereignty spread throughout the Middle East and the Balkans and left its influence on the tables and kitchens of many countries. Its demise came this century with World War I.

Just as politically the countries of the Middle East were conquered and reconquered and the geographical boundaries changed, so the culture and customs of the conquerors were imposed on the conquered. Conversely, the conquerors absorbed and were influenced by the subject nations. This applied to social and even religious customs and not least to culinary matters. Thus, foods claimed as indigenous to one country are found throughout the whole region, sometimes adapted to local supplies, conditions and tastes.

The food of the Middle East is largely vegetarian and so is well in tune with the tastes today of young health-conscious Australians. It uses lots of herbs and spices such as coriander, both fresh and seed varieties, turmeric, cumin and cardamom. Important foods are lentils, pita (bread), burghul (cracked wheat), couscous, aubergines, spinach and yoghurt.

Couscous is the national dish of Morocco, Tunisia and Algeria and is also popular in other Middle Eastern countries. Served with meat, fish, vegetables, yoghurt, or as a sweet, it is a fine semolina made from hard wheat grain. The traditional time-consuming preparation and steaming in a couscoussier is now no longer necessary as prepared couscous can be bought in a packet from Middle Eastern and Greek groceries.

Cooking is typically done on top of the stove, as originally there were only public ovens. Dishes still tend to be simmered slowly on top of the stove and meat, lentils and vegetables are cooked almost to the point of falling apart. Meat is also cooked over charcoal, whether it be a large portion of lamb or small pieces called kebab. Barbe-

cuing is a popular way of cooking meat in the Middle East and so suits the Australian way of life perfectly. Lamb and chicken are the most commonly used meats.

For Muslims, meat must be halal, that is, the animal must have been ritually killed according to Muslim law and it must have been alive and healthy before slaughter. Such meat is supplied through designated butchers. Pork is forbidden, as is blood, so grilling meat is a way of preventing blood from being ingested. Alcohol is prohibited, so you won't find wine used in traditional recipes. Vegetables are often stuffed with minced meat and often flavoured with spices and nuts.

A very thin pastry, made by rolling and pulling a ball of dough until it has stretched to a paper-like, almost transparent, thinness, is used often in the sweets of the Middle East. Today in Australia, we can buy ready prepared filo pastry.

Flavours and aromas reflect a love of sensual pleasures, but the use of cheaper meats in small quantities, cooked slowly, stems from the poverty of many people and the paucity of expensive ingredients.

Festivals observed in Australia and emanating from Middle Eastern homelands are both religious and secular and are marked by serving special dishes or, indeed, by abstaining from food, as in the Muslim observance of the fast of Ramadan (Ramazan in Turkey and Iran). Ramadan falls in the ninth month of the Muslim lunar year. No food is eaten between sunrise and sunset. These times are not casually estimated, but checked in a daily newspaper. If this is not possible, there is an old custom of putting together a black and a white thread and holding them against the light; if they cannot be distinguished from each other, then it is deemed to be sunset. Breakfast is taken well before sunrise, followed by fasting for the rest of the day; dinner taken after sunset is quite substantial. At the end of Ramadan, the fast is broken by a festive family meal.

A special sweet served during Ramadan is ataif, pancakes dipped in syrup, sprinkled with pistachios and layered with cream, or stuffed with walnuts, cinnamon and sugar. It is a sweet for all happy occasions. Another is amardine, an apricot pudding.

Turkish friends told us of the Sugar Festival which is celebrated thirty days after Ramadan and lasts for three days. It is a time for giving gifts. Children, for example, receive lollies and chocolates.

The Meat Festival falls two months and ten days later and lasts for three days, during which sheep are ritually slaughtered and distributed to the Turkish community.

Lent is observed by Christians from the Middle East for forty days before Easter. No meat is eaten on Wednesdays and Fridays and some do not even eat fish. Lenten dishes using lentils and spinach are tasty and substantial and soups are filling and satisfying.

Easter is the most important of the holy days. On Good Friday, a spinach and lentil soup is served. On Easter Sunday, a lavish

meal is served and can comprise mezze, often served with drinks, baked fish, kibbe, lamb dishes, vegetables, home-made cheeses or Lebanese cheeses from the deli.

Christmas is marked by feasting and families getting together. The most common offering is biscuits and coffee.

Engagements and weddings are occasions for special foods, among them ataif and kahk bi loz or almond bracelets. The birth of a son is marked by visits from relatives and friends. Guests are offered meghlie, a ceremonial rice pudding.

The Persian New Year (Now Rouz) is an ancient and joyous festival which, in Iran, lasts for fourteen days and marks the beginning of spring and new life. Here, it is observed on the first day only, 21 March. If it falls on a week day, when men are working, then it is left to the women and children to celebrate. They congregate at a club and bring plates of national dishes. For example, at Mount Druitt in Sydney, welfare workers organise a community feast at the Red Cross rooms. Traditionally, there were seven types of food whose names in the vernacular begin with 's' associated with Now Rooz: apples, garlic, dried unripe grapes, green wheat or barley, vinegar, a sweet pudding and rice in which was hidden a coin. These symbolised the food and fortune that would come to each house in the coming year.

HARIRA

The soup served at the breaking of the fast of Ramadan. The addition of meat will make it a meal in itself.

• SERVES 6 •

100 g chick peas
150 g haricot beans
150 g lentils
4 medium-sized tomatoes, peeled and chopped
1 large onion, chopped
salt and pepper
2 teaspoons turmeric
juice of 1 lemon
2 tablespoons cornflour
½ small bunch of coriander, finely chopped
½ small bunch of parsley, finely chopped

Wash and soak chick peas, beans and lentils overnight. Drain. Place the chick peas and beans in a large saucepan, cover with cold water, bring to the boil and simmer until tender. Add the lentils and continue to cook until these are tender. Add the tomatoes and onions and some more water. Season to taste with salt and pepper, turmeric and lemon juice, and simmer for 20 minutes.

In a small saucepan, add cornflour to 300 ml of cold water and beat to a smooth paste. Add some liquid from the soup and stir gently over a low flame until the mixture boils. Add the coriander and parsley and pour into the soup. You may need to add more liquid and seasoning.

FATTOUSH

Bread is respected throughout the Middle East since, for centuries, people's existence chiefly depended on it. Not a morsel of bread was wasted and, when the bread dried, it was used in a salad. This is a wonderful salad with an unusual texture.

• SERVES 8 •

2 small pieces of pitta bread
2 cos lettuce, washed and dried
1 bunch radishes, sliced
4 spring onions, chopped
2 Lebanese cucumbers, sliced
3 medium tomatoes, cut into wedges
¼ cup parsley, finely chopped
¼ cup fresh mint, chopped

Dressing

¼ cup lemon juice
¼ cup olive oil
salt and freshly ground pepper

Crisp the pitta bread in the oven. Break into bite-sized pieces and place in a large bowl. Add the lettuce leaves, radishes, spring onions, cucumbers and tomatoes. Mix in the parsley and mint. Combine the dressing ingredients and pour over the salad.

Salatit Humus

In this salad, garlic and herbs enhance the flavour of the humble chick pea. It has a moreish flavour.

• SERVES 4–6 •

1 cup chick peas, soaked for 2–3 hours
2 cups prepared vegetable stock
juice of 1 large lemon
¼ cup olive oil
¼ cup chopped coriander leaves
¼ cup chopped parsley
1 clove garlic, crushed
salt and pepper
2 tablespoons chopped onion

Boil the chick peas in vegetable stock for approximately 45 minutes until cooked but not too soft. Drain.

Mix the herbs with lemon juice, olive oil, garlic and seasoning. On a large platter, arrange the chick peas, sprinkle with chopped onion and pour over the dressing.

Gazar bi Kamon

A fiery spicy carrot dip with a Moroccan flavour. Because of its vibrant colour, it looks great as a dip, mezze or accompaniment to any dish.

• SERVES 6 •

500 g carrots
1 teaspoon paprika
¼ teaspoon cayenne
2 teaspoons cumin
3 tablespoons lemon juice or wine vinegar
4 tablespoons olive oil
1–2 cloves garlic, crushed
½ teaspoon grated ginger
salt and pepper
chopped parsley to garnish

Peel the carrots and boil until soft but not mushy. Drain and put in a food processor with the rest of the ingredients and blend until smooth.

TAHINA

A favourite Middle Eastern dip which can be served with fresh vegetables and pitta bread, or as a sauce on a shwarma sandwich. To achieve a creamy smooth finish, it is best made in an electric blender.

• SERVES 6 •

2–3 cloves garlic, crushed with salt
juice of 2 lemons, or more to taste
150 ml tahina paste
½ cup chopped parsley

Put all the ingredients in a food processor or blender and mix to a smooth creamy paste. Serve in a bowl dusted with paprika or cumin, and sprinkled with olive oil.

KUKUYE KADOU

Omelettes come in almost as many versions as there are countries. Italy has frittata, in Spain it is tortilla. Kukuye is a Persian recipe using zucchini.

• SERVES 4–6 •

6 eggs
1 large onion, finely chopped
8 zucchinis, thinly sliced
1 teaspoon turmeric
½ teaspoon cumin
salt and pepper
2 tablespoons clarified butter

Beat the eggs in a large mixing bowl. Add onion, zucchinis, spices and seasoning, and mix well.

In a large frying pan, heat the clarified butter over a low heat. Pour the egg mixture over the hot butter, cover and cook for about 7 minutes. The omelette is ready when it is firm. Slice into wedges and serve with a mixed herb salad.

LAHMA MESHWI

This tender cut of lamb, scented with herbs, is versatile and easy to prepare. It is equally delicious pan fried or barbecued.

• SERVES 6 •

6 fillets of lamb (boneless lamb loin chops)
½ cup chopped fresh coriander
½ cup chopped parsley
2 tablespoons chopped mint
1 teaspoon cumin
few chilli flakes
1 tablespoon lemon juice
6 tablespoons olive oil
2 cloves garlic, crushed
2 cups prepared couscous (follow instructions on packet)

Mix the herbs, spices, lemon juice, olive oil and garlic. Cover the lamb fillets with the marinade and leave in the refrigerator for 3–4 hours.

Barbecue or pan fry the fillets in a heavy based frypan. They are best when the centres are still pink. To serve, place couscous in the centre of the platter and surround with thinly sliced lamb fillets.

OHF TAPUZIM

Chicken cooked with oranges is a popular Israeli dish. Israeli cooking combines elements of both European and Middle Eastern styles whereby many dishes combine meat and fruit to achieve a sharp and pronounced contrast of flavours.

• SERVES 4 •

1 medium chicken
juice of 1 orange
2 tablespoons brown sugar
1 tablespoon peanut or other flavourless oil
1 tablespoon French mustard
1 teaspoon ground coriander
½ teaspoon ground cumin
¼ teaspoon cayenne pepper or dash of Tabasco sauce
1 orange, peeled, pitted and cut into segments
peel of 1 orange, cut into fine strips and blanched in boiling water for 5 minutes

Quarter the chicken and place it in a large bowl. Combine the orange juice, sugar, oil, mustard and spices. Mix well and pour over the chicken pieces. Marinate the chicken in the refrigerator for approximately 2 hours. Arrange the marinated chicken pieces in a baking dish and bake in a preheated oven at 200°C for half an hour. Baste the chicken pieces with the pan juices, reduce the heat to 180°C and cook for a further 15 minutes.

Remove the cooked chicken from the pan and keep warm until ready to serve. Separate the fat from the pan juices. In a saucepan, reduce the pan juices by one-third, add the orange segments and blanched orange peel, and cook for 1 minute.

Arrange the chicken on a platter, pour over the sauce and position the orange segments attractively on top.

BSTILLA

Cooked for special occasions, this dish combines a variety of flavours. Traditionally, pigeon is used and a special dough is prepared which requires great skill. Here, we have substituted chicken for pigeon and filo pastry provides an excellent alternative for the cook in a hurry.

• SERVES 4 •

2 chicken breasts and 4 boneless chicken thighs, cut into small pieces
8 sheets of filo pastry
clarified butter or oil

Marinade

1 teaspoon saffron threads, dissolved in 1 tablespoon hot water
2 tablespoons lemon juice
1 small Spanish onion, finely chopped
½ teaspoon ground ginger
2 tablespoons chopped continental parsley
1 tablespoon chopped fresh coriander
salt and pepper
3 tablespoons olive oil
2 eggs, well beaten

Combine all marinade ingredients, except the eggs. Marinate the diced chicken in this mixture for 12 hours or overnight.

In a large frypan, gently fry the chicken pieces for 15 minutes. Remove the chicken and reduce the liquid by half. Pour the well-beaten eggs on to the reduced liquid and cook to form a light omelette.

Line a baking dish with 5 layers of filo, brushing each layer with clarified butter or oil. Place the chicken pieces on top of the filo. Cover the chicken with the omelette. Place 3 layers of filo on top, again brushing each layer with clarified butter or oil. Bake in a hot oven (200°C) for 30 minutes.

MUSHAT B'GHALIM

St Peter's fish, native to the sea of Galilee, resembles white fleshed perch. Schnapper is a good substitute. As in biblical days, the fish is prepared in a simple way, with onion, parsley and lemon juice, and grilled or barbecued.

• SERVES 6 •

1 kg schnapper
½ cup finely chopped onion
3 tablespoons chopped parsley
4 tablespoons lemon juice
2 tablespoons olive oil
salt and freshly ground pepper

Combine the onion, parsley, lemon juice and oil in a mixing bowl. Rub the fish all over with this mixture. Bake or barbecue the fish for 20 minutes, turning over half way through cooking and basting with any remaining marinade. Sprinkle with salt and pepper before serving.

SAMAK BI TAHINI

A large schnapper filled with couscous and flavoured with herbs and spices makes a perfect focal point for festive occasions or dinner parties. Using packeted couscous makes this dish simple to prepare while still a feast for the eye and palate.

• SERVES 6 •

1 large schnapper
1 cup prepared couscous (follow instructions on packet)
4 tablespoons chopped parsley
4 tablespoons chopped fresh coriander
4 teaspoons chilli flakes
1 tablespoon lemon juice
2 tablespoons olive oil
1 clove garlic, crushed
salt and pepper
sprigs of coriander
4 tablespoons pine nuts, lightly fried in oil

Sauce

2 egg yolks
¼ cup lemon juice
½ cup tahina
salt and pepper

In a large bowl, mix the prepared couscous, herbs, spices, lemon juice, 1 tablespoon olive oil and garlic.

Stuff the cavity of the fish with the mixture. Secure with wooden skewers or toothpicks. Brush the fish with 1 tablespoon olive oil. Sprinkle with salt and pepper, and score in diagonal strips. Bake in a preheated oven (180°C) for 20 minutes.

To make the sauce, combine egg yolks and lemon juice in a double saucepan. Cook, whisking all the time, until the mixture becomes light and frothy. Remove from the heat and add tahina and salt and pepper to taste.

Arrange the whole baked schnapper on a platter, decorate with sprigs of coriander and pine nuts, and surround the fish with the sauce.

SAMAK MESHWI

In this fish recipe, we have used a typical North African marinade, chermoulla. This marinade combines favoured Middle Eastern herbs and spices but different ones may be substituted: chopped onion instead of garlic; marjoram, tarragon or basil may be added.

• SERVES 6 •

6 king fish steaks or jewfish cutlets

Marinade

½ cup finely chopped fresh coriander
½ cup finely chopped fresh parsley
2 large cloves garlic, crushed
2 teaspoons cumin
2 teaspoons paprika
1 dash Tabasco sauce
juice of 2 lemons
¾ cup olive oil
salt and pepper

Mix all the marinade ingredients in a large dish. Make diagonal slits in the fish. Place in the marinade and leave it for 2 hours or longer. Make sure the marinade is rubbed over all of the fish.

The best way to cook this fish is directly over a charcoal fire. If this is not possible, you can place it under the griller for 4–5 minutes per side. The flesh should be juicy and its skin brown and crispy.

BAMIA BE TAMAT

Okra and tomatoes make a rich and satisfying vegetable dish. The natural thickness and savoury taste of okra lend a unique flavour to many stews.

• SERVES 4–6 •

3 tablespoons cooking oil
3 small onions, finely chopped
4 medium sized tomatoes, peeled and chopped
2 tablespoons tomato paste
1 teaspoon cumin
salt and pepper
250 g okra

Heat the oil in a saucepan. Fry the onion until soft and translucent. Add tomatoes, tomato paste, cumin and seasoning. Cook over a low heat for about 10 minutes, stirring frequently until the mixture is cooked and well amalgamated. Wash and dry the okra. Add to the tomato mixture and cook for 7–10 minutes. Be careful not to overcook the okra as it will become stringy.

SALATIT KOUSA

With every Middle Eastern meal, there is an exotic salad or vegetable accompaniment. Boiled vegetables are nearly always dressed with olive oil and lemon. We have used zucchini here and fried it quickly instead of boiling it.

• SERVES 6 •

500 g zucchini, sliced lengthways
3 tablespoons olive oil
2 tablespoons raisins or sultanas
2 tablespoons toasted pine nuts
1 clove garlic, crushed
juice of 1 lemon
salt and pepper
chopped mint for decoration

Fry the zucchini quickly in olive oil for 2–3 minutes. Transfer to a serving bowl. Add the raisins, pine nuts, garlic, lemon juice, salt and pepper. Allow to cool and serve sprinkled with chopped mint.

AMARDINE

During Ramadan, a traditional sweet is made from dried sheets of apricot called amardine. We have substituted dried apricots for amardine in our recipe for this delicious Middle Eastern soufflé-like dessert.

• SERVES 6 •

150 g dried apricots
juice from 2 oranges
4 egg yolks
200 g sugar
50 g semolina
100 g ground almonds
4 egg whites
icing sugar for dusting

Cook the dried apricots and orange juice on a low heat until the apricots become soft and half the orange juice evaporates. Leave aside until cold. Purée the cooked apricots and remaining juice in a food processor.

Beat the egg yolks and 150 g sugar in a bowl. Make sure that all the sugar is dissolved and the mixture is light and fluffy. Fold the semolina and ground almonds gently through this egg yolk mixture, then add the apricot purée.

Beat the egg whites until peaks start forming. Now add the 50 g sugar and beat for a further few seconds. Gently fold the beaten egg whites into the egg yolk and apricot mixture. When it is mixed thoroughly, pour into a baking tin lined with baking parchment and well-greased with butter. Bake in the oven at 180°C for 45 minutes. When cooked, invert the cake onto a platter and dust liberally with icing sugar.

SVARJEIL

This neglected fruit was once very popular in Europe and the Middle East. It is now gaining in popularity again. Raw quinces have a tart, astringent flavour. When cooked in syrup, they become sweet and aromatic.

• SERVES 4 •

2 quinces	*1 cup water*
½ cup sugar	*1 whole vanilla bean*

Peel and core the quinces, and cut into eight pieces. Reserve the peel and cores, place in a muslin cloth and tie securely.

In a deep saucepan, dissolve the sugar in water and boil for 5 minutes. Add the quince segments, the muslin bag and the vanilla bean. Cook on a low heat for 20 minutes or until the quinces are soft. Serve cold with the syrup in which they have been cooked.

SHARBAT ANAR

Sorbet is a water ice whose basic ingredients are fruit juice purée and sugar syrup. The Chinese introduced it to the Middle East and the name derives from the Turkish 'chorbet'. Pomegranate conjures up all the romance of the Arabian Nights. If fresh pomegranates are not available, use pomegranate syrup, available from Middle Eastern food stores.

• SERVES 6–8 •

2 cups sugar	*juice of 4 pomegranates*
2 cups water	

Boil the water with the sugar for 15 minutes until syrupy. Allow to cool. Mix the pomegranate juice and the syrup in a bowl that is freezer proof. Freeze until solid. Transfer to a blender and blend for a few seconds until mushy. Serve in glasses.

ORGAMI

Japanese

JAPAN and Australia, while having very different histories and cultural backgrounds, have in common societies which enjoy freedom and democracy. Although relations go back approximately one hundred years (the first Japanese Consulate was opened in Sydney in 1897) they have developed tremendously in the last ten years.

Currently, the total population of Japanese in Australia is approximately 12,000 of whom some 5,000 are permanent residents. Nearly all live in the capital cities, with the largest populations in Sydney and Melbourne. Some come here as representatives of large Japanese commercial, construction and engineering organisations and often stay for a period of three to five years only; others have established small businesses as importers of clothing and food and, of course, as restaurateurs.

Most of the Japanese residents, permanent or temporary, live on the lower North Shore in Sydney and that is where you will find shops offering Japanese cooking ingredients and take-away foods. There are some fifty restaurants at this time in the city and northern suburbs. In Melbourne, the Japanese seem to prefer the south-eastern areas, with pockets in Box Hill, where the first Japanese supermarket was opened. Japanese food marts are located in Prahran and Elsternwick and restaurants are everywhere, particularly in the city and in South Yarra.

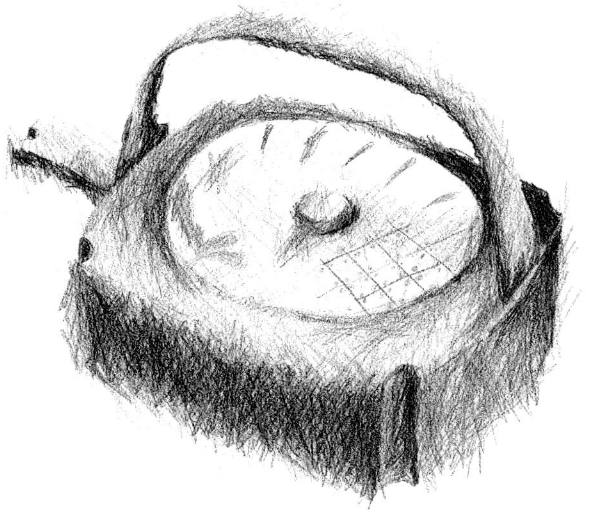

The arrival of Japanese tourists in large numbers has resulted in the proliferation of restaurants and noodle bars, especially on Queensland's Gold Coast, which has long been a favourite venue for Japanese holidaymakers.

The respect which Japanese cooking holds for purity stems from Shintoism, the ancient religion of Japan. Shintoism venerates nature, which it deems to be sacred and pure. This is reflected in the way food is chosen and presented. The Japanese demand quality and appearance of food that is worthy of the best that nature can offer — shiny, freshly caught fish, full ripe fruit, clear sake wine, snow-white rice. To attempt to elaborate on such perfection is considered unnecessary and even in bad taste. When Buddhism was introduced to Japan in the sixth century, it blended harmoniously with Shintoism. At the same time, each religion retained its individual forms of worship and ceremonies. Today, Japanese people may marry in Shinto shrines but are often buried with Buddhist rites.

Surrounded by oceans, Japan has long depended on the sea for much of its food. Fish is a main element in the Japanese diet and is eaten in a variety of ways — raw, steamed, fried, boiled and grilled.

In Japan, raw fish is a highly refined delicacy and it is no longer considered unusual in Australia. Raw fish is served either as sashimi, in thinly sliced strips with a special dipping sauce and wasabi or horseradish, or as sushi. For sushi, the ingredients other than raw fish are vinegared rice, seaweed, vegetables and wasabi.

Besides fish, other products of the sea are eaten, including nori, a type of seaweed which has been dried and pressed flat, frequently eaten with rice, and kamaboko, a hard gelatin of ground fish flesh. Prawns, squid, eel, sea urchin and kelp are also popular.

A Japanese meal is a communion with nature. As we eat these foods, we are aware of them in their natural form as living and

growing products of the earth and the sea. Quantity is measured to avoid satiety and, hence, a possible feeling of revulsion.

Japanese cuisine reveals considerable regional variation. One delight of travelling in Japan is the obento or lunch box of rice, vegetables, meat or fish sold at most train stations. Obento vary from region to region in content, style and packaging, and offer a taste of local cooking. In Australia, obento can now be bought at major fish markets and also from dial-a-meal services.

The Japanese use hashi or chopsticks for the whole meal. For this reason, food is served in manageable bite-sized pieces and hashi are also perfect for use with the dipping sauces. Etiquette precludes reaching with chopsticks beyond a nearby dish or transferring one's chopsticks from one side dish to another without first taking rice. Chopstick rests keep the food-holding ends of the chopsticks off the table top or cloth. These appealing little rests come in all designs, from fish, flowers and figures of children to birds and ships, and in materials of wood, ceramic or silver. They make an attractive accompaniment to a table setting.

Many Japanese meals are one-pot dishes called nabemono and include sukiyaki and shabu-shabu. Each person takes a selection from a platter of artistically arranged ingredients and cooks it in a pot standing in the middle of the table on a heating unit. Individual bowls of dipping sauce and condiments are conveniently placed near each guest or family member.

Japanese cooking has made deep inroads into modern Australian culinary and eating habits. Our hotels are importing chefs to implement Japanese menus which are sought after more and more. Our chefs are going to Japan to learn the philosophy and methods of its cuisine. Even French chefs and restaurants are incorporating Japanese-style foods into their kitchens and menus; they are increasingly using raw and lightly cooked ingredients to allow the natural flavours to come through.

Although festivals are not publicly celebrated here, the ceremonial foods associated with them are available in Australia all the year round in Japanese food shops. Thus you can buy mochi (rice cakes), miso, white radish, azuki beans and all sorts of fish products.

New Year's Holiday or Oshogatsu, from 1 to 3 January, is Japan's most important holiday. It is a time when all the family comes together to celebrate the New Year. Before and after the holidays, trains throughout the country are jammed with people going to and from their ancestral homes.

On New Year's Eve, many Japanese dress up in their best kimonos and go to a local shrine or temple to offer prayers for health and happiness in the coming year. On the stroke of midnight, the temple bells ring in the New Year 108 times (joya-no-kane). Special foods are served at home during New Year in a multi-tiered, lacquered box called a jubako. They are known collectively as osechi-ryori and include mochi, ozóni (rice cake soup), red beans, kelp, fish roe and marinated fish. Vinegared daikon (white radish) mixed with shaved carrots provides the traditional red and white colour combination for the festive table. This would be as eagerly awaited a meal as Christmas lunch is for Australians.

The mochi, or more correctly kagami-mochi, is also an offering to the gods. It consists of two mochi, one on top of the other, and is placed in the tokonoma or alcove of the main room of the house where a shrine is usually found.

Toshikoshi means seeing out the old year and seeing in the new. Toshikoshi soba are long, thin buckwheat noodles eaten on New Year's Eve to symbolise longevity.

On 3 February, the eve of Setsubun, the first day of spring, roasted soybeans are scattered in and around the house to drive out sickness and misfortune.

The most important summer festival is Obon, or the Festival of the Dead, which is celebrated from 13 to 16 August. It is Buddhist in origin and honours the memory of one's ancestors. Tradition has it that the spirits of the deceased return home at this time of the year. Houses are carefully cleaned, family graves are swept and symbolic offerings of food are placed before the family altar in every home.

OZÓNI

The Japanese New Year is greeted with a toast of otoso (spiced sake) and hot soup filled with a variety of ingredients. The word ozóni mainly evokes a picture of mochi (rice cakes) in some kind of soup.

• SERVES 6 •

dashi or chicken stock
250 g boned chicken
salt to taste
1 medium carrot
1 teaspoon light soy sauce
6 mochi cakes (available at Japanese grocery stores)
small bunch watercress, washed and drained

Prepare and heat 3 cups of dashi or chicken stock. Slice the chicken into thin pieces and sprinkle lightly with salt. Blanch in the stock till cooked. Drain the chicken pieces. Peel the carrot and cut into 1 cm thick rounds. Parboil till almost tender, about 10 minutes. In a soup pot, bring the strained chicken stock to the boil. Turn down the heat to keep the stock at simmering point, then add the salt and soy sauce. Meanwhile, grill the mochi cakes under a griller, making sure that they do not burn. When the surface is crisp, pierce with a fork in several spots to allow the soup to penetrate. Place the hot mochi in individual deep soup bowls and add the chicken slices and carrot rounds. Pour the simmering soup over the mochi and chicken. Decorate each soup bowl with sprigs of watercress.

MISO-SHIRU

Miso, or bean paste, is one of the most essential ingredients in Japanese cooking and the base of miso soups. Miso soups are not only easy to prepare, but they also provide a substantial amount of the adult daily requirement of protein. This version of miso soup contains chicken, shiitake mushrooms, tofu and bean sprouts.

• SERVES 6 •

4 cups water
2 tablespoons miso paste
2½ tablespoons mirin
¼ teaspoon finely grated fresh ginger
250 g chicken breast fillets, cut into 5 cm strips
6 shiitake mushrooms
6 × 2 cm cubes of tofu
3 tablespoons bean sprouts
4 spring onions cut into bite-sized pieces
pepper

Bring the water to the boil and stir in miso paste, mirin and ginger. Bring back to the boil and add the chicken pieces. Reduce heat, cover and simmer until the chicken is just cooked. Add mushrooms, tofu, bean sprouts and spring onions, and simmer for a further 5 minutes until everything is cooked. Add pepper to taste. Serve in soup bowls accompanied by boiled rice.

SASHIMI

The presentation of raw fish and meat is one of the characteristics of Japanese cooking. Preparation of sashimi is done with great care and only the freshest ingredients are used. Although the slicing and arrangement of sashimi requires skill, there is no need to be intimidated as even a moderately skilled cook can prepare a delicious and attractive plate of sashimi. Beef sashimi provides an easy introduction to sashimi dishes.

• SERVES 8 AS AN APPETIZER •

450 g fillet of beef, without any fat or sinew
salt to taste
4 teaspoons wasabi
4 tablespoons finely chopped spring onion
4 teaspoons finely grated fresh ginger
2 cucumbers
6 shiso leaves or 6 basil leaves
2 tablespoons light soy sauce mixed with
1 teaspoon mirin

Salt the fillet of beef. Quickly sear the beef on all sides over a hot charcoal fire. Plunge the meat into iced water to cool, then pat dry. Brush the fillet of beef with wasabi. Mix together the chopped spring onion and grated ginger, and press all over the beef. Slice the cucumber into thin strips. Cut the prepared beef against the grain into very thin slices. On a platter, arrange the strips of cucumber in the centre and surround them with finely sliced beef. Decorate with shiso leaves. Serve the soy sauce and mirin for dipping in a separate bowl.

TEMAKI-SUSHI

Sushi, after sashimi, is the most famous and tempting of Japanese dishes. The expert preparation of sushi takes years of practice, and home preparation cannot compare with that done at sushi restaurants. Skill in preparation, the art of presentation and dedication to the use of the freshest ingredients are the essence of good sushi.

We have provided a recipe that offers satisfactory results but is a little easier to prepare. Temaki is hand-wrapped sushi which is not as firmly or evenly packed as the kind rolled in a bamboo mat nor is it cut into bite-sized rounds. The main ingredient of all sushi is vinegared rice which is a little harder and 'chewier' than plain boiled rice. The rice is put into hot water, rather than cold water, and once cooked, it is quickly cooled. This is done by constantly tossing the rice, which affects its consistency. The Japanese use a wooden tub for cooking and tossing the rice.

• SERVES 6–8 •

Sushi rice

3½ cups short grain rice, washed
4 cups hot water
8 cm square konbu (kelp)
5½ tablespoons rice vinegar
5 tablespoons sugar
4 teaspoons sea salt

Temaki-sushi

120 g very fresh tuna fillet
120 g very fresh salmon fillet
1 small cucumber
½ avocado, not too ripe
10 sheets, 18 × 20 cm, toasted nori (seaweed paper)
60 g fresh salmon roe
10 shiso leaves
2 teaspoons wasabi
¼ cup soy sauce
1 tablespoon sake
50 g pickled ginger slices

To prepare sushi rice, put the rice in a heavy-bottomed, medium-sized pot. Pour over hot water, place konbu on top of the rice, cover and cook over a medium heat until it comes to the boil. Remove konbu, cover and cook on a very low heat for 20 minutes or until all the water has been absorbed. When the rice is cooked, let it stand in the covered pot for 15 minutes.

Meanwhile, prepare the vinegar dressing. Dissolve the sugar and salt in the vinegar over a low heat. Quickly cool the vinegar mixture. Spread the hot rice in a thin layer in a wide, shallow wooden container or any other bowl except one made of metal. To keep the grains separate, toss the rice with cutting strokes. While tossing, sprinkle vinegar dressing over the rice, a little at a time, to make sure that the rice does not become too soggy. The rice is ready when it has reached room temperature. Sushi rice must be used the same day. To keep it moist, cover with a damp cloth.

To prepare temaki-sushi, cut tuna and salmon into 8 × 1½ cm pieces. Using scissors, cut cucumber and avocado into 8 × 1½ cm pieces. Cut each nori sheet into quarters. Arrange tuna, salmon, roe, shiso, cucumber, avocado and wasabi paste on a serving platter. Arrange nori on a plate and place sushi rice in a serving bowl. Mix soy sauce and sake and place in individual small bowls for dipping.

To serve, each person assembles and wraps their own sushi rolls. On a nori sheet, place one or two tablespoons of sushi rice, top with a few ingredients and add a dab of wasabi. Then fold nori over to form a cone-shaped roll and dip lightly in soy and sake sauce. (If desired, sushi rolls can be prepared beforehand and served on a platter.) The pickled ginger is served as an accompaniment.

ARAMAKI

In the past, salt-preserved meat and fish wrapped in straw were called aramaki. Nowadays, aramaki means salted salmon. It is one of the prized gifts found in jubako, the boxes traditionally used by the Japanese to serve food in during the New Year festival. In this recipe the salmon is lightly seared and then pickled.

• SERVES 8 AS AN APPETIZER •

500 g fresh salmon fillet
salt and freshly ground pepper
1 teaspoon oil
¼ cup rice vinegar
2 tablespoons mirin
1 tablespoon light soy sauce
2 tablespoons finely chopped spring onions

Season the fish with salt and pepper. Sear the surface of the fillet in a heavy non-stick pan greased with the oil. The fish should remain raw. Remove the fish from the pan, pat dry with a paper towel and place in an oval bowl. Mix together vinegar, mirin, soy sauce and spring onions, and pour over the fish. Marinate in the refrigerator for 24 hours. To serve, drain the marinated fish, slice the fillet into thin slices and arrange neatly on a platter.

DATOMAKI

A type of fish omelette eaten at New Year celebrations. Usually, the egg is mixed with mashed fish and seasoned with soy sauce and mirin. The cooked omelette is then rolled, while still warm, in bamboo mats to firm the shape. When the omelette has cooled, the mat is removed and the roll sliced into pieces. Here, we provide a slight variation to the traditional recipe. Instead of the mashed fish, we have used slices of smoked salmon.

• SERVES 8 •

½ cup dashi or chicken stock
1 tablespoon mirin
1 tablespoon light soy sauce
8 eggs
1 teaspoon oil for frying
8 slices smoked salmon
white radish for decoration

In a large bowl, mix the dashi or chicken stock, mirin and soy sauce. In another bowl, gently beat the eggs, making sure that they do not become frothy. Pour the eggs into the mixture.

To fry the omelette, use a Japanese rectangular egg pan. If this cannot be obtained, use a shallow frypan. Wipe the frypan with some oil. Pour half the mixture into the hot frypan, and tilt the frypan to allow the mixture to spread in an even layer. When nearly cooked, spread 4 slices of salmon on top of the omelette. Tilt the pan up and, with chopsticks or spatula, roll up the omelette. Remove from the pan and wrap in a bamboo mat. Repeat this procedure with the remaining portion. After a few minutes, unwrap the omelette rolls and slice crosswise into rounds, 5 cm thick. Arrange the slices on a platter and garnish with grated white radish.

KAREI NITSUKE

Foods simmered in a half and half mixture of sake and soy sauce are popular in Japanese cooking because of their strong, piquant flavour. This recipe for flounder also works well for other flat fish such as small bream or schnapper.

• SERVES 4 •

4 fresh flounder
7 tablespoons mirin
7 tablespoons sake
1 cup dashi or chicken stock
7 tablespoons soy sauce

Ask your fishmonger to scale, gut and wash the fish, leaving the heads and tails intact. Score the tops of the fish with 3 or 4 diagonal slits. These slits allow the stock to penetrate the flesh and cook the fish faster. Mix the stock ingredients in a pot large enough to accommodate the fish. Bring the sauce to the boil. Put the fish, with the slits up, in the boiling stock. For a lid use a piece of baking parchment large enough to cover the pot. Cut a vent in the paper. Cook over a high heat for 10 minutes. Lift each fish on to a platter with a spatula, making sure that the fish does not break. Pour a little stock over the fish before serving.

ZARU-SOBA

Soba are traditional Japanese noodles made from buckwheat, eggs and the starch of root vegetables. They are available in a packet, ready for cooking, from health shops and Japanese grocery stores. Zaru-soba are chilled buckwheat noodles, sprinkled with strips of seaweed.

• SERVES 4 •

10 cups water
250 g dried buckwheat noodles
¼ cup finely shredded toasted nori (seaweed)

Sauce

2 cups dashi or chicken stock
½ cup dark soy sauce
4 tablespoons mirin
1 teaspoon sugar
4 tablespoons finely chopped spring onions
1 teaspoon wasabi

Bring 7 cups of water to the boil in a large pot. Add the noodles gradually so that the water remains on the boil. Stir slowly to prevent the noodles from sticking to the bottom of the pot. Bring to the boil again, then add 1 cup of cold water. Repeat this twice. Cook further until the noodles are cooked, but still quite firm. Drain the noodles in a colander and rinse under cold running water, rubbing vigorously with the hands to remove surface starch. Separate the strands by shaking the colander. When the noodles are well drained, arrange them on a basket plate, chill and, before serving, sprinkle with nori shreds.

Prepare the sauce by boiling together dashi or chicken stock, soy sauce, mirin and sugar. When the sauce is cold, add the finely chopped spring onions and wasabi. Serve in individual serving bowls. The noodles are then dipped in the sauce.

SAKE SARADU TSUTSUMI-YAKI

This stuffed salmon, baked in foil, derives from foods cooked traditionally either in paper or bamboo leaves. Trout and barramundi can also be prepared in this way.

• SERVES 6 •

2 salmon fillets, each 500 g
salt
4 tablespoons mirin
2 tablespoons butter
2 lemons, cut in thin slices
10 fresh shiitake mushrooms
1 cup finely chopped spring onion

Salt the fish two hours prior to cooking. Preheat the oven to 250°C. Rub the fish fillets with mirin. Spread 1 tablespoon of butter along the centre of a piece of foil, cover with half of the lemon and put 1 fillet on top. Arrange the mushrooms over the fish, sprinkle with the spring onions and cover with the second fillet. Dab with the remaining butter and place the rest of the lemon slices on top. Fold the foil, sealing tightly, and bake for 15 minutes without turning.

To serve, open the foil, place a serving plate on top of the fish, invert and remove the foil, retaining any juices on the plate.

TEMPURA

Nothing is more tempting than a basket-plate filled with lacy, golden, deep-fried fish and vegetables. Making tempura is easier when the ingredients are fresh, the temperature of the oil is constant and the batter is lumpy.

• SERVES 4 •

400 g small white-fleshed fish fillets	*1 green capsicum*
1 medium onion	*8 mushrooms*
1 medium kumera	*flour for coating*

Batter

2 egg yolks	*2 cups sifted flour*
2 cups iced water	*oil for deep frying*

Sauce

3 tablespoons mirin	*3 tablespoons soy sauce*

Pat the fish fillets dry. Cut the onion into quarters and peel the layers. Slice the kumera thinly. Cut the capsicum into wide strips. Coat all the ingredients with flour and shake off any excess.

In a mixing bowl, lightly beat the egg yolks, then add the iced water. Add the flour and mix gently just to combine the ingredients. The batter should be lumpy. In a deep pot, heat the oil until it is fairly hot. Test by dropping a small amount of batter into it. If the batter floats to the top, the temperature is right. Place a draining rack nearby.

Dip each ingredient in the batter, then place it in the hot oil. Cook for 3 minutes, then remove with a slotted spoon and place on the draining rack. Serve on a bamboo basket accompanied by the dipping sauce.

SUKIYAKI

This Japanese one-pot cooking is very famous outside Japan. In Japan, a special cast iron pot is used for sukiyaki, but in Australia an electric frying pan is often used as a substitute. A large platter with attractively arranged beef slices and vegetables is placed on the table and the dish is cooked at the table. The cooked food is then placed in individual bowls into which an egg has been broken.

• SERVES 6 •

500 g fillet of beef, finely sliced
8 fresh shiitake mushrooms
6 spring onions cut into 5 cm strips
1 bunch young spinach, washed and trimmed
half chinese cabbage, cut into strips
150 g bean sprouts
2 cups cooked rice vermicelli noodles
200 g cubed tofu
1 tablespoon oil for greasing the pan
6 eggs
4 cups boiled rice

Sauce

1 cup beef stock
¼ cup water
¼ cup sake
¼ teaspoon grated fresh ginger

Combine beef stock, water, sake and ginger in a bowl. Arrange the beef, prepared vegetables, tofu and rice noodles on a platter shortly before serving time. Give a bowl containing a raw egg to each person. Beat the raw egg lightly with a chopstick.

Rub the pan with the oil. When the pan is hot, add the beef and stir-fry until it loses its pink colour. Push the beef to one side and add all the prepared vegetables except the spinach. When the vegetables have softened slightly (do not overcook), add the sauce and simmer for 4 minutes. Now add the spinach, tofu and rice noodles, turning gently to absorb the flavour of the sauce. Serve the boiled rice and place the sukiyaki in the bowls on top of the raw egg.

YAKITORI

Chicken morsels grilled over hot charcoal and basted with a sweet soy-based sauce is one of Japan's more popular foods. The best part of the chicken for yakitori is the leg or the thigh because meat from this part of the chicken is juicier than that from the breast. Other ingredients, such as fish or vegetables, can be substituted. Yakitori is a terrific dish to serve at a barbecue party.

• SERVES 6 •

500 g boned chicken thighs or legs cut into bite-sized pieces
bamboo skewers

Sauce

7 tablespoons sake
¾ cup dark soy sauce
3 tablespoons mirin
2 tablespoons sugar

Skewer 5 pieces of chicken on each bamboo skewer. Bring all the sauce ingredients to the boil. Grill the chicken over hot charcoal for 20 minutes. Dip the chicken into the sauce and continue grilling. Repeat the dipping and grilling until the chicken meat is cooked but not over-cooked as the meat will be dry. Serve the skewers on a platter, moistening the chicken with a little of the sauce.

YAKI-SHIITAKE PONZU-AE

Fresh shiitake mushrooms should not be overcooked or they will lose their delicate flavour and will dry out.

• SERVES 4 •

4–6 shiitake mushrooms per person

Ponzu sauce

1 tablespoon lemon juice
1 tablespoon rice vinegar
1 tablespoon soy sauce
1 tablespoon mirin
1 tablespoon finely chopped spring onion

Wipe and trim the mushrooms. Grill the mushrooms, stem side up first, then cap side, for no longer than 5 minutes in all. Alternatively, the mushrooms can be fried gently on both sides in a little bit of oil for no longer than 3 minutes. Mix together all other ingredients. Place the hot mushrooms on a platter and pour the sauce on top.

HORENSO GOMA-AE

This salad is made from fresh young spinach. It is served cold and goes with almost anything. Like many other Japanese dishes, the seasoning is derived from the dashi (stock made from sea kelp) and mirin which is sweet cooking sake. Most Japanese grocery stores stock these ingredients, but if they cannot be easily obtained, substitute chicken stock and sake.

• SERVES 4 •

2 bunches of trimmed, washed and partly cooked spinach
½ cup dashi or chicken stock
1 teaspoon mirin
3 teaspoons light soy sauce
1 teaspoon sesame seeds, toasted

In a small saucepan, bring the dashi or chicken stock to the boil, reduce the heat, then add the mirin and soy sauce. Cool the liquid and transfer to a serving bowl. Chop the spinach into 5 cm long pieces and place in the bowl with the liquid. Chill in the refrigerator. Before serving, sprinkle with the toasted sesame seeds.

NAMASU

Daikon (white radish) and carrot, marinated in rice vinegar and lemon juice, make an appetizing dish to enjoy with hot rice, meat or fish.

• SERVES 4 •

1 medium daikon, peeled
1 large carrot, peeled
1 teaspoon salt
¼ cup rice vinegar
1 tablespoon lemon juice
1 teaspoon mirin

Coarsely shred the daikon and carrot and place with salt in a colander. Drain for 5 minutes, then transfer to a serving bowl. Mix the rice vinegar, mirin and lemon juice, and pour it over the daikon and carrot. Refrigerated, this dish will keep for up to two days.

SIGURE

This miso relish is a good topping for rice, vegetables or bread. Miso is a fermented bean paste that is used in a variety of ways in Japanese cooking.

3 tablespoons oil
½ cup chopped spring onions
½ cup chopped eggplant
1 cup miso
¼ teaspoon grated ginger

Fry the spring onions, then add the eggplant and cook slowly until the vegetables become soft. Add the miso and cook for 3 minutes. Stir in the ginger and remove from the stove. Cool and use as a condiment.

ISU KURIMU

Green tea, the most important of Japanese beverages, gives this ice cream a delicate and distinctive flavour.

• SERVES 6 •

½ litre milk
¼ litre cream
200 g sugar
2 tablespoons Japanese green tea
6 egg yolks

Place the milk, cream and 100 g sugar in a saucepan and bring to the boil. Add the green tea, cover and leave to infuse for 30 minutes.

Place the egg yolks and the remaining sugar in a bowl and beat with a whisk or electric beater until the mixture becomes pale. Bring the milk and cream mixture back to the boil and pour a little of it into the bowl with the egg mixture, whisking constantly as the rest of the liquid is added. Strain through a fine mesh strainer into the saucepan. Cook on a very low heat, stirring all the time with a wooden spoon until the mixture slightly thickens. This will take about 20 minutes. When the mixture coats the back of the wooden spoon, it is ready. Remove from the heat. Cool over iced water, stirring from time to time, then pour into an ice cream churn. In a good quality ice cream churn it will take about 1–1½ hours to form into the consistency of ice cream.

紹興酒

Asian

FREEDOM Plaza is in Cabramatta, an outer suburb to the west of Sydney. A beautiful mall planted with golden trees, it is approached through a magnificent arch bearing the words 'Liberty' and 'Democracy' and a message in the languages of three of the communities who live in Cabramatta. Over the arch are the words, in English, 'The world is for us to share and to respect'. These are beautiful thoughts expressing the hopes and ideals of people who aspire to live harmoniously together in the land of their adoption.

Our choice of the three countries to represent Asia was based on the same criteria we used elsewhere in the book.

CHINESE

Even before the gold rush days of the 1850s, the Chinese came to Australia as servants, artisans and labourers, as indentured workers and free immigrants. Many more came during the gold rushes, working at Ballarat, Bendigo and other mining sites in Victoria, and in places such as Bathurst and Braidwood in New South Wales, and moving on to Cooktown in Queensland and Pine Creek in the Northern Territory as discoveries were made there.

They were peaceful, industrious and frugal, sending gold back to their families in China where they intended and hoped to return rather than settle permanently in Australia. This fact and the competition they provided caused resentment among the European settlers who, sadly, attacked and destroyed Chinese camps at Lambing Flats in Victoria in 1861. The government then moved to restrict the numbers of Chinese in the state.

After the gold rushes, Chinese miners moved to the cities and towns where they took up market-gardening, cabinet-making and laundering. Chinese traditional medicine was practised by herbalists whose patrons included Europeans as well as Chinese. Earlier this century, the Chinese in Queensland became successful banana growers.

In spite of discrimination and the adoption of the White Australia Policy in 1901, Chinese culture was nurtured and survived. The community staged traditional operas and lion and dragon dances, and set up schools to maintain some Chinese learning. Most children, however, went to English-speaking schools set up by the Catholic and Protestant churches, to which faiths many converted. Some still worshipped at Chinese temples the gods of Mercy, Loyalty and Wealth.

They concerned themselves with events in their distant fatherland, such as its wartime resistance, giving financial and moral support and identifying with the political changes. After World War II, an open door policy was adopted here; finally, in 1973, the White Australia Policy was abandoned and Chinese immigration increased. Many of these new residents — from China, Hong Kong, Singapore and Papua New Guinea — and locally born Chinese have a high degree of education and have entered the professions and higher levels of commerce.

The largest number of Chinese are to be

found in Sydney, followed by Melbourne, but they also live in every other city and, indeed, throughout the country. Each city has its Chinatown with restaurants, speciality shops, clubs, medical centres. It plays a vital role in community support and cultural activity, especially at festival times. Here, most weddings and parties take place. In Melbourne, it is in Little Bourke Street where its history goes back to the 1850s; in Sydney it started in Dixon Street and spread throughout the Haymarket. In 1980, Henry T'sang designed the arches which mark each end of Dixon Street, making it into a mall. Lions guard the magnificent red portals of the archways.

To Chinatown in Cabramatta, in Sydney's west, have come Chinese from China, Indo-China and South East Asia. Here, in the shopping centre, is a concentration of restaurants and shops with rare cooking ingredients, dried fish and fruits and vegetables not seen elsewhere and grown locally.

The Chinese follow religions as varied as the countries in which they have settled. Buddhism, Islam, Taoism, Christianity (an increasing influence on Chinese in Australia) and Confucianism, which is rather a code of ethics than a religion. It teaches moral principles of behaviour, the rules governing nature and forbearance as a way to success.

Taoism dating back to the fourth century B.C. is a philosophy which stresses balance in everything, yin and yang, a counterbalance between hot and cold, man and nature, and in food, a balance in the groups of foods and the methods of cooking.

Chinese food has been popular for many decades in Australia and Chinese restaurants are to be found in every city, suburb and country town. Today, some have become quite grand and elegant, and new styles of eating have been introduced. Yum cha, traditionally the time in the morning, around 11.30, for drinking tea and eating small delicacies, has developed into a popular form of lunch. Trolleys laden with many sorts of fried and steamed snacks are wheeled around to the tables and copious amounts of fragrant tea are drunk for pleasure and to aid digestion. Chinese cuisine embodies both the culinary and the medicinal. Banquets are important as the sharing of foods is an integral part of any celebration. The Chinese believe in the magic of numbers, so an even number of dishes is served on joyous occasions to bring good luck, good health and prosperity. At funerals, an uneven number is served.

Rice is the staple food and noodles are eaten frequently in all households.

Today, Hong Kong chefs come to Australia on special working visits to keep local people up to date with contemporary developments in Chinese cuisine. Competitions among Chinese chefs ensure high standards of quality and innovation.

The main festivals are observed by all Chinese regardless of religion. More recent arrivals here tend to be homesick so cling nostalgically to old traditions and customs.

New Year is calculated according to the lunar calendar. It falls around February and lasts for fifteen days. It is celebrated throughout Australia with dragon and lion dances in front of the shops in Chinatown and with fireworks. Worshippers visit their temples.

Small potted cumquat trees are bought in Chinatown as gifts or to decorate the home. The word cumquat means 'golden luck'.

The Moon or Mid-Autumn Festival is on the fifteenth day of the eighth lunar month when the moon is at its biggest and brightest. The story is that a beautiful woman stole a potion from her husband. She was turned into a fairy and flew to the moon. The festival is marked by family reunions. Paper lanterns are lit, delighted children walk around with them and the full moon is admired. The festive food is moon cakes, round pastries filled with red bean paste and egg yolk or fruits and preserves. They can be bought from Chinese stores.

Ching Ming Festival held in mid-spring honours the ancestors. Incense and paper money, obtainable in Chinatown, are burned. Food, usually that favoured by the departed, is offered to the ancestors and their graves are visited.

The Dragon Boat Festival commemorates a Chinese poet of some two thousand years ago. He was a national hero who as a political protest threw himself into the sea. Local fishermen beat the water with their paddles to stop fish from attacking him. It is said, too, that people threw dumplings into the sea so that the fish would eat them and not the body of the poet. Today, in April or May, depending on the lunar calendar, the Dragon Boat Race is held and rice dumplings are eaten. Many Chinese people make these at home but they can also be bought from Asian shops.

The first Dragon Boat Race was held in Sydney in 1984 and Melbourne followed the next year. It is now an annual event, attracting participants from outside Australia and non-Chinese also. Competing teams bring their boats and decorations from Asia. Dragon heads and tails are affixed to the boats. To bring them to life symbolically, incense and firecrackers are lit and a Taoist priest paints dots on the dragons' eyes. Sacrificial paper money is put in the dragons' mouths and thrown into the water to ward off evil spirits.

VIETNAMESE

From the second century B.C., Vietnam has been subject to influences from China, India, France, the United States and, more recently, Communism. Through all these, Vietnamese culture has survived.

This century, Vietnam has suffered political and military oppression. After World War II, from 1946 to 1954, Communist forces struggled against France for their independence, encouraged by the victory of Mao Tse-tung against Chiang Kai-shek in China. With the defeat of France, Vietnam was divided: the North became Communist and many Vietnamese, eighty per cent of them Catholic, fled to the South, which under Diem was backed by the United States.

The second Indo-China War, 1960 to 1975, between the North and South ended with reunification under Ho Chi Minh. American support was withdrawn with dire economic and social outcomes. So began the exodus of the 'boat people' on a frequently dangerous journey to freedom.

Australia accepted these people as political refugees on humanitarian grounds and later,

under a family migration program, took in more for the size of the host population than any other country in the world.

The term 'Vietnamese' covers two distinct ethnic groups: Viets and Chinese who have been living in Vietnam. They were the second largest group of immigrants into Australia in the late 1970s and early 1980s. In this country, they have tended to be politically conservative being suspicious of leftist politics.

There are settlements of Vietnamese throughout Australia, with most in Sydney, Melbourne and the other capital cities. Few are in country areas as they look to compatriots for support and are especially concerned to live near centres of education for their children. Even those who are market gardeners grow their produce close to the outer suburbs where they live.

In Melbourne, the largest concentration of Vietnamese settlers is in Footscray and in Richmond where the shops in Victoria Street reflect their life-style. In Sydney, they live in Marrickville, Tempe and Dulwich Hill, which are closer to the city, and in the outer western suburbs of Cabramatta, Liverpool, Fairfield and Birrong, where rents are lower and housing is easier to get. There are food markets in Glebe Point Road, Glebe, and in Chinatown in Sydney, and restaurants are everywhere.

Some few Vietnamese are engaged in the professions with qualifications acquired here or at home but recognised here. Some have gone into small business in the food or clothing trades; most are process workers or labourers. The women are often employed in outwork for the clothing industry or in Vietnamese restaurants and food shops.

The Vietnamese place a high value on education and students are encouraged to study hard to gain a tertiary education, seen as the key to entry into the professions. At the same time, community schools, mostly during weekends, teach Vietnamese language, history and dance to keep the culture alive and to help communication between children and their elders. Without this, the tendency of the young to adopt Western values leads to tensions within the family. The Vietnamese language is a subject for university entrance and is taught at some high schools and at tertiary level as part of university courses in Asian studies.

There are many formal and informal networks which give the support that is no longer provided by the divided family, some of whose members may still be in camps overseas awaiting the chance to join those who have managed to come here. Vietnamese welfare offices advise newcomers about government services such as housing, employment and legal aid, and give emotional as well as practical support.

Vietnamese culture is based on Buddhist thought, for some of Chinese origin on Confucianism and, since the seventeenth century, Christianity. It is centred on spirituality in the home, with veneration of ancestors. In Australia, Mahayana Buddhism and Catholicism are the main religions. Few people are active members of religious organisations, but attend Buddhist and Christian places of worship for special festivals and celebrations. The more recent arrival of some Vietnamese Catholic priests has been a help and spiritual comfort to Catholics. Some Buddhist monks have also arrived in recent years and are now serving in temples in all states, tending to the needs, religious and cultural, of their followers with particular outreach to youth. There are temples in Sydney at Smithfield and Fairfield where the Phap Bao Pagoda has been built in traditional Vietnamese architectural style.

The Vietnamese are careful about choosing an auspicious day for almost any event. They study the calendar and consult soothsayers, usually the temple monks, to find the right day to marry, to open a business, to buy a house, to travel, to go for a job interview. Some wear amulets to ward off evil.

Because of the Chinese ethnicity of so many Vietnamese, some festivals are similar to those observed by the Chinese population. Têt is New Year and, according to the lunar calendar, falls between late January and mid-February. In Vietnam, the pleasure-loving southerners celebrate the festival for a week but, here, only the first two days are faithfully observed as work and business must go on. During the week before Têt, stalls are set up in malls, such as the one at Cabramatta, where various foods can be bought in anticipation of visits from family and friends. By the last day of the year, all preparations must be completed, all debts must be settled and new clothes and shoes bought for the children.

On the eve of Têt, incense is burned and, on the first and second days, visitors are received and visits are made to others. Devout Buddhists go to the temple. At home, guests are served tea and sweets, multi-coloured confections, preserved fruits such as tamarind, pineapple and melon, peanut brittle, dried sweet coconut. Sweets are also given as gifts. Parents give the children Li Xi money for New Year, wishing them good health and success in their studies. Nevertheless, as there is no public or school holiday here at this time, school children stay away from school so as not to miss the fun.

The Moon Festival falls in September and is marked by eating moon cakes. These are very sweet and can be bought at this time at any of the Asian shops.

Buddha's Birthday, Phat Ban, falls in May/June. Buddhists go to the temple and pray for those who died for freedom. At the temple, vegetarian food is served to the worshippers — rice, mushrooms, fresh roe, rice noodles.

The Fall of Saigon in 1975 is observed on 8 April. Vietnamese shops fly flags and Vietnamese organisations hold gatherings where speeches are made confirming the anti-communist stance of political refugees.

Birthdays used to be celebrated at Têt but, in Australia today, they are observed on the actual anniversary of birth. Weddings are lavish affairs. The ceremony takes place in front of an ancestral altar, bearing a picture of the ancestors. Wedding banquets are in western style and the quite amazing many-tiered wedding cakes are elaborately iced and decorated.

THAI

'Beauty without grace is a violet without a smell.'

Thailand's history of relative political stability and prosperity, and its freedom from colonisation, has meant a small degree of emigration and at the same time the preservation of its culture and respect for, even veneration of, the royal family. Its keen perception of the working of politics and its unique understanding of diplomacy have insulated it from the wars, invasions, guerilla forays and internecine strife that have racked South East Asia. Apart from some isolated protests against any erosion of its democratic style of government, Thailand has stood free and undisturbed.

In character, the Thai people are kind, charming, polite and tolerant. Their behaviour is gracious and friendly and they have an innate love of beauty.

Migration to Australia started with small numbers in the 1960s, steadily increasing until there are now some thousands of Thais here. Many of them are temporary residents attached to embassies or consulates, tourist and airline offices and private or government sponsored students. The permanent population consists of those who have established businesses here and those who have intermarried with Australians.

Their presence is not conspicuous in any one area. They live where the Australian partner may have lived and students cluster around the universities. Their low profile is not reflected in the number of Thai restaurants which are countless and immensely popular, not only among Thais but also among the Australian born. Apart from the exotic aura, the food is light, yet spicy, aromatic and decorative. Wherever there is a restaurant area, there will be one or more serving Thai food.

The Thais here are predominantly Theravada Buddhists. They do not worship Buddha as a god, but many keep images to remind them of him. Meditation is practised to obtain purity of mind. Temples or wats are supported and visited on special days. These are in Stanmore, Leumeah and Wiseman's Ferry in New South Wales, at Serpentine in Western Australia, in Springvale in Melbourne and Thebarton in Adelaide. The monks at the wats rely for sustenance on the food offered by their followers. They must eat whatever is placed in their bowls, which is why their style of Buddhism is not vegetarian. The food is usually something that the giver thinks a revered ancestor would have liked.

Festivals are celebrated with joy and pleasure, this quality of 'sanuk' contributing to the well-being of participants and friends. New Year falls around mid-April and is marked by visiting the temples to offer food to the monks in thanksgiving and in memory of ancestors. It is associated with Song Kran, a happy festival, when water is thrown to ensure a bountiful year of rain. In Thailand, it is the hot season and people shower one another with water. Here, images of Buddha are bathed and young people sprinkle water over the hands of elders and monks in respect — and drench one another with water in fun!

A popular dish at this time is kao chaey, fluffy jasmine rice, shredded beef and stuffed chillis, served with iced jasmine water.

Loy Krathong is the Festival of Floating Leaf Cups. In November, during full moon, when most of the soil and mud have settled to the bottom of the river and the water is clean, moon, sky and water are seen to be clear at the same time. The festival is dedicated to the Goddess of Water, Mae Kongka, and the Goddess of Rice, Mae Bhosob. The custom is to put food, incense

and money, together with a lighted candle, in the cups of leaves and to float them down the river. It is a yearly offering to the water spirits and symbolises a floating away of sins. For today's sophisticates, it is more a floating away of cares. This pretty ceremony is performed here in parks where there is a pond or lake.

Wan Phra is the day on which some Thai people make their weekly visit to the temple. The day is calculated according to the lunar calendar, but here the visits are made on Sunday, the only free day, with gifts of rice, food to go with it, a dessert or fruit and flowers.

Visakh Day, in the middle of May, the sixth lunar month, commemorates the birthday of Buddha, the day he became enlightened and the day of his death. The traditional dish for this day is steamed sticky rice, with banana and black-eyed beans, wrapped in banana leaves.

Buddhist Lent begins in July. A special dessert of sticky rice, shredded coconut and syrup, wrapped in banana leaves, is served. Only two meals a day are eaten; neither meat nor alcohol is taken. To truly observe the precepts means to sleep on the floor instead of a bed, to meditate and to visit the temple each week. It is a period of abstinence and self-denial.

Sart, on the other hand, signifies the time of abundance of food and is celebrated in September to mark the harvest of young rice. A special dessert is krayasart which consists of peanuts, sesame seeds, rice puffs, palm sugar and honey, mixed together to make a crunchy sweet.

The Phapa ceremony occurs during Lent in September/October when the monks are presented with food and new saffron-coloured robes. The King's birthday, two weeks earlier, is publicly celebrated in some festive way, sometimes with a communal picnic and kite-flying.

At weddings, food is chosen that symbolises happiness and prosperity. A customary dessert, foi-thong or golden threads, is made with duck-egg yolks and is sweet and sugary.

Another dish for special occasions is mee-grob, crispy noodles, signifying long life. Anything golden or fragrant is a favourite choice for celebrations.

TOM KHAR GAI

Galangal is a root similar in appearance to ginger, but with a milder taste, used often in Thai cooking. Combined with the different spices, it gives this chicken soup a spicy and delicious flavour.

• SERVES 4 •

1½ cans coconut milk
1–2 cups chicken stock
8–10 kaffiar lime leaves
4–6 pieces galangal, peeled and sliced
2 stalks lemon grass
2 tablespoons lemon juice
2 tablespoons fish sauce
2 tablespoons dark chilli paste
3–4 chicken breast fillets cut into small pieces
50 g fresh straw mushrooms
fresh coriander
fresh red chillies, cut into strips

Put chicken stock and coconut milk in a saucepan, bring to the boil and add lime leaves, galangal, lemon grass, lemon juice, fish sauce and dark chilli paste. Stir well. Bring to the boil again, add chicken pieces and simmer until the chicken is cooked. Add the straw mushrooms.

Serve in a bowl, while very hot, garnished with coriander leaves and strips of red chilli.

GAI HOR FUN

Stir-fried chicken, bean sprouts, ginger and spring onions make a tasty filling for sheets of fresh rice noodles. These noodles can be obtained from Asian supermarkets. This is a popular yum cha dish.

• SERVES 4 •

2 tablespoons peanut oil
1 tablespoon shredded fresh ginger
½ cup chopped spring onions
200 g chicken breasts, shredded
½ cup bean sprouts
250 g fresh rice sheet noodles
3 tablespoons soy sauce
½ teaspoon sesame oil
½ cup fresh coriander sprigs

Heat the oil in a frypan or wok. Stir fry the ginger and spring onions. Add the chicken and fry for several minutes until cooked. Add the bean sprouts and cook for a further half minute.

Lay out the rice noodles, cut into 10 cm squares and place 1 tablespoon of the filling on each. Roll up the pancakes and place on an ovenproof serving platter. Mix the soy sauce with sesame oil and sprinkle over the pancakes. Cover and heat in a moderate oven for 10 minutes.

Serve, decorated with sprigs of fresh coriander.

PHO

Traditional Vietnamese beef noodle soup, with a side plate of basil, bean sprouts, freshly sliced chillies, tomatoes and lime, makes a substantial meal.

• SERVES 6 •

Soup

1 kg beef bones
700 g brisket of beef
3 litres water
small knob of ginger
salt to taste
4 tablespoons chopped lemon grass
2 star-anise tied in a piece of muslin
1 medium brown onion, finely sliced
1 clove garlic, finely chopped
4 tablespoons Vietnamese fish sauce
250 g rice noodles
3 tablespoons finely chopped spring onions
3 tablespoons chopped fresh coriander

Accompaniment

3 limes, cut in half
6 cherry tomatoes, cut in half
3 tablespoons shredded Vietnamese basil
2 teaspoons sliced fresh chillies
2 cups fresh bean sprouts, washed and trimmed

Place the bones, ginger and salt in the water. Bring to the boil and remove the foam from the surface. Simmer for 30 minutes. Add the brisket of beef and cook slowly until the meat is tender, about 3 hours. Again skim the foam from the surface, making sure that the broth is clear. Half an hour before the beef is cooked, add the lemon grass, star-anise, onion, garlic and fish sauce. Just before serving, cook the rice noodles in boiling water for 1 minute.

To serve, slice the beef brisket. Place a portion of noodles in each bowl, cover with the broth and top with slices of beef. Sprinkle with spring onions and fresh coriander. On a plate arrange the bean sprouts, chillies, tomatoes, limes and basil. Serve as an accompaniment to the soup.

YUM NEAU

A spicy Thai beef salad which is excellent as a starter for any meal or as a buffet dish for a summer luncheon.

• SERVES 4 •

2 medium thick rump steaks
2 cloves garlic
2–3 coriander roots
6 fresh red chillies
2 tablespoons lemon juice
2 tablespoons fish sauce
1 lettuce
¼ cup mint leaves
¼ cup coriander leaves
1 punnet of cherry tomatoes

Char-grill the steak rare and slice thinly. Pound garlic, coriander roots and 1–2 chillis until well mixed, then add lemon juice and fish sauce. Combine well. Pour over prepared beef.

Arrange dry lettuce leaves on a platter, place beef on top and decorate with mint, tomatoes, coriander and remaining chillies, seeded and sliced lengthways.

TORD MUN PLA

These little Thai fish cakes look harmless but deliver quite a punch, while tempting your taste buds for the next course. The hot and spicy flavour combines well with the cucumber salad.

• SERVES 4 •

Fish cakes

½ kg red fish fillets
1 tablespoon red curry paste
1 egg
½ tablespoon fish sauce
8 kaffar lime leaves, soaked in hot water and shredded
6–8 stringless beans, thinly sliced
1 bunch basil
oil for frying

Remove bones and cut fish into large pieces. Place in a food processor and add curry paste, egg and fish sauce. Blend on high speed until fish is finely minced. Transfer fish mixture to a medium-sized bowl. Add lime leaves, beans and shredded basil. Mix by hand until the ingredients are well combined, and keep on working for about 5 minutes. Divide the mixture into 12 equal portions. Form into round shapes and flatten.

Heat oil in a wok. Cook the fish cakes until fluffy and golden. Pat dry with a paper towel. Serve with spicy cucumber salad.

Salad

1 cucumber, peeled, seeded and sliced thinly
100 ml of white wine vinegar
2 tablespoons sugar
pinch of salt
1 clove garlic
½ small red chilli
1 tablespoon crushed roasted peanuts

Dissolve sugar in vinegar over a low heat, then add salt. When cool, add pounded chilli and garlic. Pour on top of cucumber and top with nuts.

CHAR YU

Garfish is plentiful nearly all the year round in Australian fish markets. It has a sweet white flesh and is delicious served Chinese style.

• SERVES 4 •

8 medium-sized garfish
salt and pepper
cornflour
peanut oil
8 slices fresh ginger
2 tablespoons soy sauce
2 stalks spring onions, chopped

Wash and dry the scaled garfish. Slap each fish with a large, flat-sided mallet. This enables the middle bone to be removed easily.

Roll in cornflour mixed with salt and pepper. While heating a heavy based frying pan, rub the base with a piece of peeled ginger. (This will give a delicate fragrance to the fish). Add enough peanut oil to cover the base of the frying pan, then add the sliced ginger. When the oil is hot, add the garfish and fry quickly until they are crisp and golden on one side. Turn the fish over. When both sides are crisp, tip out excess oil, reduce the heat to low, and add the soy sauce and spring onions. Cook for 30 seconds and serve immediately.

CHING GNE GEONG CHOONG

Bream and ocean perch have juicy white flesh. The Chinese prefer to steam fish as it retains the moisture. You can also cook it covered in the oven. Here it is served with shallots and snow pea shoots.

• SERVES 4 •

2 medium-sized whole bream or ocean perch (scaled and gutted)

Sauce

1 teaspoon peanut oil
1 tablespoon soy sauce
2 tablespoons chopped shallots
1 teaspoon finely grated fresh ginger

Accompaniment

1 tablespoon peanut oil
1 teaspoon finely grated fresh ginger
2 tablespoons chopped shallots
2 cups snow pea shoots
1 tablespoon soy sauce
1 teaspoon sesame oil

Cut diagonal slashes in the fish. Mix together the sauce ingredients and pour over the fish. Place on an ovenproof platter. Cover with foil and cook in a moderate oven for 15 minutes or until cooked. Alternatively, place the fish in a steamer, cover with the sauce and cook for 15 minutes.

Meanwhile, heat the peanut oil in a wok or saucepan and gently fry the ginger and shallots till soft. Add the snow pea shoots and stir fry for 1 minute. Toss in soy sauce and sesame oil and remove from heat. Arrange the cooked snow pea shoots around the fish.

CA KHO THOM

This tangy dish of fried John Dory fillets and freshly sliced pineapple is heightened in flavour by the use of Vietnamese fish sauce.

• SERVES 4 •

600 g John Dory fillets
2 tablespoons flour
salt and pepper to taste
2 tablespoons oil
½ fresh pineapple, peeled and sliced
2 tablespoons chopped spring onions
4 tablespoons Vietnamese fish sauce

Caramelized sugar

1 tablespoon sugar
2 tablespoons water
1 tablespoon lemon juice

Prepare caramelized sugar by melting sugar in a small saucepan until it becomes golden in colour. Add water and cook until the sugar is well mixed with the water. Add the lemon juice and remove from heat.

Coat the fish fillets with flour mixed with salt and pepper. Heat the oil in a frying pan or wok. Fry the fish until it is cooked. Transfer the fish to a hot platter, tip off excess oil and stir fry the pineapple, spring onions and fish sauce. Cook for 2 minutes. Arrange the pineapple slices and spring onions on top of the fish fillets and pour over the caramelized sugar.

RAU MUONG XAO

Stir-fried spinach and tender fillet steak make this delicious Vietnamese dish suitable for any occasion.

• SERVES 4 •

250 g fillet steak
1 medium-sized onion, finely chopped
1 teaspoon pepper
1½ tablespoons fish sauce
1 tablespoon cornflour
1 large tomato
1 bunch English spinach
2 tablespoons oil
1 clove garlic, finely chopped

Slice the fillet steak into thin strips. Toss the meat in onion, ½ teaspoon pepper, ½ tablespoon fish sauce and the cornflour. Remove seeds and skin from the tomato and slice thinly. Wash and dry the spinach well.

Heat 1 tablespoon oil in a frying pan. Throw in the spinach and garlic and stir fry for 1 minute. Add the remaining fish sauce and the tomato slices and cook for a further minute. Transfer the vegetables to a warm platter. Heat the remaining oil in the frying pan, add the meat slices and stir fry for 3 minutes. Place the meat over the spinach and sprinkle with pepper.

GA XAO LAN

Turmeric and light coconut milk give the chicken in this Vietnamese dish a lovely golden colour and a fragrant aroma.

• SERVES 4 •

500 g chicken breasts
1 cup coconut milk
1½ cups hot water
2 tablespoons oil
1 clove garlic, crushed
1 medium brown onion, cut into strips
1½ tablespoons turmeric
1 tablespoon chopped lemon grass
1 teaspoon black bean sauce
fresh coriander for garnish

Mix the coconut milk with hot water. Cut the chicken breasts into finger-sized strips. Heat oil in a large frying pan. Add onion and garlic. Toss in the chicken pieces and stir fry until they change colour. Add the coconut milk, turmeric, lemon grass and black bean sauce, and cook over a moderate heat for about 15 minutes or until the chicken is cooked. Arrange the cooked chicken on a warm platter, pour over the sauce and garnish with sprigs of coriander.

GANG KEOW WARN GAI

A classic Thai curry. It is well worth the effort making this tasty curry paste rather than buying the commercial type.

• SERVES 4–6 •

2 cans coconut milk
6 chicken breast fillets, cut into finger-sized strips
3–4 red chillis
1 bunch fresh basil
1 red capsicum, cut into small strips

Green curry paste

10–20 red and green chillis
4 pieces galangal
¼ cup chopped lemon grass
1 teaspoon chopped coriander root
1½ teaspoons coriander seeds
½ tablespoon cumin
1 onion
3–4 cloves garlic
½ tablespoon shrimp paste
1 tablespoon palm sugar
2–3 tablespoons fish sauce
10 kaffiar lime leaves

Pound or blend all the ingredients for the curry paste, except the fish sauce, palm sugar and lime leaves, till well mixed. In a pan, heat one-quarter of the coconut milk (the creamy part). Add curry paste, fish sauce, palm sugar and lime leaves, and cook for a few minutes.

In a medium-sized saucepan, place the rest of the coconut milk and the chicken pieces, and bring to the boil. Add the prepared mixture and simmer for 20 minutes until chicken is cooked.

Just before serving, bring to the boil and add fresh basil, capsicum and chillies. Serve with steamed jasmine rice.

HOI SIN GAI

This is an old, well-tried Chinese recipe, but still a great favourite. It is simple to make, yet the flavour is delicious. It is best served with boiled rice and chopped coriander or parsley.

• SERVES 4 •

500 g chicken fillets (breasts or thighs)
1 tablespoon cornflour
salt and pepper to taste
1 egg white, beaten but not stiff
½ tablespoon soy sauce
1 tablespoon sherry
2 tablespoons sugar
1 teaspoon sesame oil
cooking oil
1 clove garlic, crushed
2 tablespoons hoi sin sauce

Cut the chicken fillets into bite-sized pieces. Dip into cornflour mixed with salt, pepper and egg white. Leave for 10 minutes. Mix together the soy sauce, sherry, sugar and sesame oil.

Heat a wok till quite hot with just enough oil to cover it (the chicken should smoke slightly when added). Add chicken pieces and cook for 1 minute. Transfer to a plate. Place crushed garlic and hoi sin sauce in the wok, cook for 10 seconds, then add the chicken and the soy mixture. When the sauce has coated the chicken, remove and serve.

COM THO GA

This is a special Vietnamese way of cooking rice. Here we serve it with chicken and vegetables.

• SERVES 4 •

Steamed rice

2 cups rice
2 cups water
¼ teaspoon salt
1 teaspoon sugar
1 tablespoon oil

Chicken and vegetables

10 Chinese dried mushrooms
200 g fresh button mushrooms
1 large onion
2 medium-sized zucchinis
1 red capsicum
4 chicken breasts
4 tablespoons oil
½ teaspoon salt
2 cloves garlic, finely chopped
1 tablespoon sugar
2 tablespoons soy sauce
½ teaspoon sesame oil
2 tablespoons fish sauce
1 tablespoon fresh coriander sprigs
1 tablespoon chopped spring onion

Rinse the rice well, with several changes of water. Place the rice in a heat-resistant bowl and cover with water, 1.5 cm above the rice. Mix in the salt, sugar and oil. Cover the rice, place over a saucepan filled with water and steam the rice for about 1 hour or until cooked. Make sure that the water in the saucepan does not evaporate.

Soak the Chinese mushrooms for half an hour. Remove the stems and cut them into quarters. Cut all the vegetables, except the button mushrooms, into finger-sized strips. Slice the chicken breast in the same way.

Heat 2 tablespoons of oil in a large frying pan or wok. Add half the salt, garlic and onion. Stir fry until the onion becomes translucent. Add the sugar and Chinese mushrooms and stir fry on a low heat for 2 minutes. Increase the heat and add all the other vegetables. Cook for 2 minutes and remove all the vegetables. Heat the remaining oil and the rest of the salt, onion and garlic. Stir fry until the onion becomes translucent, then toss in the chicken pieces. Cook the chicken for approximately 10 minutes, then add the cooked vegetables, soy sauce, sesame oil and fish sauce. Cook for 1 minute, mixing well. Garnish with fresh coriander sprigs and spring onion. Serve with the special steamed rice.

CONG CHAO MIAN

This is fried noodles with spring onions, Cantonese style. It is easy to cook and a splendid accompaniment to any meal. Fresh egg noodles can be obtained at Asian food shops.

• SERVES 4 •

450 g fresh thin egg noodles
12 spring onions, finely chopped
1 teaspoon salt
3 tablespoons peanut oil
2 tablespoons dark Chinese vinegar

Plunge the noodles into a large saucepan of boiling salted water for 2 minutes, then drain thoroughly To the drained noodles, add the chopped shallots and salt.

In a non-stick 30 cm frying pan, heat the oil. When it is hot, add the noodles and press to the shape of the pan. Turn the heat down very low and continue to cook for 10 minutes. If the noodle mixture seems to be drying out, sprinkle it with cold water. Carefully turn the cake of noodles over and continue cooking till the other side is brown. Sprinkle the noodles with dark Chinese vinegar and season to taste. Slide on to a platter and serve.

WANGFUJING LENG MIAN

This is a tasty Chinese cold noodle dish. The soft noodles contrast with the refreshing cucumbers, and it is easy to prepare.

• SERVES 4 •

450 g fresh Chinese egg noodles
1 tablespoon sesame oil
4 cucumbers
175 g fresh bean sprouts

Sauce

½ tablespoon finely chopped garlic
½ tablespoon finely chopped fresh ginger
2 teaspoons soy sauce
1 tablespoon dark soy sauce
1 tablespoon sugar
2 tablespoons peanut butter
1 tablespoon peanut oil
1 tablespoon white rice vinegar
2 teaspoons chilli oil

Boil the noodles for 3 minutes and drain thoroughly. Rinse in cold water and immediately toss in sesame oil.

Peel and cut the cucumbers in half lengthways and, using a teaspoon, remove the seeds. Slice the cucumber halves into fine long shreds. Rinse the bean sprouts and drain thoroughly.

Mix the sauce ingredients together in a blender. Just before serving, toss the noodles with the sauce, then add the cucumbers and bean sprouts.

DONGGU CHAO CAI

This is a delightful combination of cabbage and mushrooms, stir fried, both popular vegetables in Chinese cooking.

• SERVES 4 •

25 g dried or 200 g fresh straw mushrooms
1 small Chinese cabbage
2 tablespoons peanut oil
1 tablespoon finely chopped fresh ginger
2 teaspoons sherry
2 teaspoons soy sauce
2 teaspoons sesame oil

If you are using dried mushrooms, soak them in warm water for a half hour, or until soft. Rinse, drain and slice. If using fresh mushrooms, wipe with a damp paper towel and slice thinly. Slice the cabbage into long thin shreds.

Heat a wok or large frying pan until hot. Add the peanut oil and, when heated, the ginger. Stir fry for 30 seconds, then add the mushrooms and cabbage. Fry for a further minute, then add the sherry and soy sauce. Stir fry for 2–3 minutes or until cooked. Slide onto a platter and sprinkle with sesame oil.

FOI-THONG

Golden threads, as this Thai dessert is called, symbolises happiness and wealth. Because of its sweetness and meaning, it is traditionally served at weddings and other celebrations. It is delicious with sliced fresh fruit such as mangoes or pineapple.

• SERVES 4 •

2 cups sugar
6 egg yolks (if possible from duck eggs)
shredded coconut

In a wok, heat sugar with 1½ cups of water, stirring until sugar is dissolved, then boil for 5 minutes. Whisk yolks until well mixed. Pour about a quarter of the egg mixture into a piping bag fitted with a 2 mm nozzle, keeping a finger over the opening. Release opening over the boiling syrup and pipe the yolk with a circular motion. Scoop out cooked egg with a mesh skimmer and set aside on a platter. Repeat until all the mixture has been used. Cover and chill. Arrange the golden threads on four dessert plates and sprinkle with shredded coconut.

KHAO NIEO KAEO

Made with glutinous rice which is available from Asian food stores, this Thai dessert is ideal served with fresh mangoes or bananas, combined with passionfruit.

• SERVES 4–6 •

1 cup glutinous rice
1 cup tinned coconut cream
2 tablespoons sugar

Wash the rice and soak in cold water overnight. Drain and steam for 30–40 minutes, or until the rice is tender. Pour the coconut cream, mixed with the sugar, over the warm rice and allow to steep for 30 minutes. Serve with sliced fruit.

BU SEE PIN GUO

A light and mouth-watering way to serve apples, this Chinese dish is tempting even to those who never touch dessert.

• SERVES 4–6 •

4 firm delicious apples
1 tablespoon lemon juice
4 tablespoons sesame seeds
cornflour
iced water
1 teaspoon red wine vinegar
peanut or vegetable oil
½ cup water
1½ cups sugar

Peel and core the apples, cut into quarters and sprinkle with lemon juice, making sure they are well coated to prevent discolouration.

Place the sesame seeds in a frying pan and cook over a moderate heat until toasted but not burnt. Set aside.

Place the apple slices in a dish and coat with flour, shaking off any excess.

Rub a large serving dish with oil. Have ready two bowls of iced water and the vinegar.

Heat enough oil for deep frying in a wok or deep-fryer and when it is very hot add the apple slices. Cook for about 5 minutes or until golden brown but not mushy. Drain.

Place ½ cup water and the sugar in a saucepan and cook on a high heat, stirring constantly until the sugar spins a thread. To test the consistency of the syrup, spoon a few drops into a basin of iced water. The consistency is correct if the syrup hardens immediately. Stir the vinegar into the syrup and add the apple quarters. Coat with the syrup, then sprinkle with sesame seeds.

Place in the oiled dish and serve with the second bowl of iced water. Each slice is then dipped in the iced water before it is eaten.

Recipe Index